What Caesar Did for My Salad

Also by the author

Red Herrings and White Elephants
Black Sheep and Lame Ducks
Phantom Hitchhikers and Decoy Ducks
Loch Ness Monsters and Raining Frogs
Pop Goes the Weasel
The Old Dog and Duck

What Caesar Did for My Salad

The Curious Stories Behind Our Favorite Foods

ALBERT JACK

A PERIGEE BOOK

A PERIGEE BOOK
Published by the Penguin Group
Penguin Group (USA) Inc.
375 Hudson Street, New York, New York 10014, USA

Penguin Group (Canada), 90 Eglinton Avenue East, Suite 700, Toronto, Ontario M4P 2Y3, Canada
(a division of Pearson Penguin Canada Inc.)
Penguin Books Ltd., 80 Strand, London WC2R 0RL, England
Penguin Group Ireland, 25 St. Stephen's Green, Dublin 2, Ireland (a division of Penguin Books Ltd.)
Penguin Group (Australia), 250 Camberwell Road, Camberwell, Victoria 3124, Australia
(a division of Pearson Australia Group Pty. Ltd.)
Penguin Books India Pvt. Ltd., 11 Community Centre, Panchsheel Park, New Delhi—110 017, India
Penguin Group (NZ), 67 Apollo Drive, Rosedale, Auckland 0632, New Zealand
(a division of Pearson New Zealand Ltd.)
Penguin Books (South Africa) (Pty.) Ltd., 24 Sturdee Avenue, Rosebank, Johannesburg 2196,
South Africa

Penguin Books Ltd., Registered Offices: 80 Strand, London WC2R 0RL, England

While the author has made every effort to provide accurate telephone numbers and Internet addresses
at the time of publication, neither the publisher nor the author assumes any responsibility for errors or
for changes that occur after publication. Further, the publisher does not have any control over and
does not assume any responsibility for author or third-party websites or their content.

WHAT CAESAR DID FOR MY SALAD

First American edition: September 2011
Originally published in Great Britain by Particular Books in 2010.

Perigee hardcover ISBN: 978-0-399-53690-8

PRINTED IN THE UNITED STATES OF AMERICA
10   9   8   7   6   5   4   3   2   1

Most Perigee books are available at special quantity discounts for bulk purchases for sales promotions,
premiums, fund-raising, or educational use. Special books, or book excerpts, can also be created to fit
specific needs. For details, write: Special Markets, Penguin Group (USA) Inc., 375 Hudson Street,
New York, New York 10014.

This book is dedicated to all cooks everywhere.
What would we do without you?

Contents

Acknowledgments

Thanks in the first place should go to chef Liam Tomlin for all the advice and encouragement during the early days. Not to mention access to the best food-history library I have ever seen. Thank you, Chef! Also to the lovely Jan Tomlin, who enthused and encouraged and kept giving me other new ideas to go and look up. Dimo Papachristodoulou, my favorite Mexican, helped, too, as did Candice Kalil with her angry pasta, and thank you, Celeste Perry, for allowing me to use your restaurant in Cape Town as an office. For further ideas and research kindly provided from those across the world, thanks to Louise De Jager in Australia and Jessica Roher in South Africa.

Peter Gordon returned to the team this year with the now famous Morecambe and Wise incident. One Saturday morning, two years ago, as I stayed with him for a few days en route from America to South Africa, we were so engrossed in discussing this book that it was after midday before we realized we were both still in our pajamas. Although at the kitchen table, mind you, and not in bed like Morecambe and Wise.

And finally I would like to thank my team at Penguin, especially my editor, Maria Gagliano. And then in no particular order: Christina Lundy, Angela Januzzi, and Jennifer Eck. Thank you all.

Introduction

Food is just as entitled to a proper history as castles, wars, kings, queens, art, literature, or the bubonic plague. But the book world is now so saturated with celebrity chefs trying to show the working woman or man how to rub garlic on a ciabatta or break lime leaves over a piece of raw fish that we've lost sight of many of our best-loved dishes, not to mention the stories behind them showing how they became such classics in the first place. And while I don't swear at incompetent sous-chefs for a living—I don't in fact know one end of a pork loin from its elbow—I do love history, and I especially love food. The history behind our favorite dishes is fascinating and full of surprises—from the Buddha's obsession with **porridge** to the dying playwright Molière dosing himself with **Parmesan** rather than medicine (it didn't work, in case you're wondering). It's also sadly overlooked, and so I wanted to find out more.

In the Monty Python film *The Life of Brian*, the would-be rebels ask: "What have the Romans ever done for us?" Well, one unexpected answer I discovered in my research is that, among many other things, they invented **fast food**. Instead of cooking, you could dash out from your high-rise apartment (they invented those, too) to your nearest street vendor to grab some takeout. It's amazing to see how much food has changed yet how it has stayed the same: how the peasants of the Middle Ages scraped by on sludgy **pease pudding** (healthier fare, even so, than the meat-rich dishes of their wealthy overlords), while today's modern-day peasant, the penniless student, survives on the tastier but not dissimilar **baked beans** on toast.

This dish, as I discovered, might well hail from France—an

offshoot of **cassoulet**, their classic bean stew—and that country, with a bit of help from Italy, has had a huge influence on European cooking. But rather than just explaining how cooking techniques have evolved over the centuries, I wanted to tell the stories about the people behind the food we eat every day. Who was **Margherita**, for instance, and why was the world's most famous pizza named after her? And what about **Suzette**: why do pancakes flambéed in Grand Marnier bear her name? We've all enjoyed **peach Melba** at some point, or spread some butter on a piece of **Melba toast**, so wouldn't it be a great idea to tell the story of the demanding diva, Dame Nellie Melba, for whom these dishes were created? And, of course, no history of food would be complete without the tale of how that inveterate gambler the Earl of **Sandwich** came up with the snack that bears his name and now forms the mainstay of every lunchbox and **buffet**.

Once I'd started my research, all sorts of intriguing questions kept popping up. Why do we call our favorite kinds of coffee **espresso** or **cappuccino**, for instance? Did medieval Turkish soldiers really invent the **shish kebab** by threading bits of meat onto their swords and balancing them on top of their campfires? What exactly does **horseradish sauce** have to do with our equine friends? Turn a few more pages and you'll find the answers to all these questions and many more.

You can look up a dish or type of food in the index or just turn to a relevant "meal." As you'll see, I have structured this book around the eating day, starting with a chapter on breakfast and ending up with cheese as the final course for dinner. These days we eat all kinds of foods at all times of day, and so the chapters aren't completely rigorous in their organization: appetizers are fairly interchangeable with starters, for instance.

The meals we eat and when we eat them have shifted over the years to reflect our increasing mobility and changing lifestyle. But they can still be a reflection of who we are. For example, everybody knows what breakfast is and, in that sense, we are all the same. If you call it "brunch," then you should probably get up earlier.

Do you call your midday meal "lunch"? If so, you are probably middle class, reasonably well off, and would spend all afternoon over it if you didn't have to go back to work. If you call it a "business lunch," then you've clearly no intention of going back at all.

Interestingly, this is actually the meal with the longest pedigree. At the beginning of the sixteenth century, the main meal of the day took place at around 11:00 a.m., for rich and poor alike, and was called "dinner," thanks to the Old French word *disner*, deriving in turn from *desjeuner* and meaning "to break the fast" (as well as providing the modern French word for "breakfast").

The day ended with "supper" or, as it came to be known in England, "tea," which was a light snack eaten as the sun went down and just before everybody went to bed. The introduction of artificial light meant that meals no longer had to take place in daylight hours: generally the richer you were, the more candles you could afford and the later you ate dinner (i.e., the main meal of the day).

Incidentally, if you call a meal with friends a "dinner party," then you probably also call lunch "lunch." But you should definitely be wary of guests who throw their keys into a bowl when they arrive. The last time that happened I ended up with my own set.

As you make your way through this book, you will see how food has affected the course of history (the Boston Tea Party, for example, or the Irish Potato Famine) and how it has, in turn, been affected by history. You'll see, for instance, how Prohibition brought out the resourcefulness of American chefs, in the form of various dishes from **Caesar salad** to **fruit cocktail**;

and how the rising price of **pepper** was the real reason behind Columbus's voyage to America. And interspersed among the entries on food you'll find everyday phrases relating to the things we eat, and the stories behind them, from **just desserts** to **humble pie**.

En route, you may be interested to discover how many national dishes actually turn out to come from somewhere entirely different: those all-American favorites the **hamburger** and the **hot dog** are, in fact (ahem), German; and France's beloved **croissant** actually hails from Austria. You'll also see what lengths people go to during times of war to rechristen a dish so that it *isn't* associated with a particular country—hence "hot dog" instead of the German-sounding **frankfurter**, or **Salisbury steak** instead of "hamburger."

So, dear readers, a cookbook this is not. But while the chefs among you will learn little here about how to assemble a particular dish, you might enjoy the stories of culinary invention. Meanwhile, less confident cooks should be happy to discover just how many of the world's best-loved dishes arose as the result of mistakes or missing ingredients.

I've enjoyed researching and writing this book enormously and I hope you find it a satisfying read. I'd love to hear your thoughts and your own food-history stories, so why not contact me at caesar@albertjack.com. Inevitably, there wasn't room to include every dish I wanted to cover in this book, but you never know—there might be a second sitting . . .

Albert Jack
May 2010
Cape Town

1

Breakfast

Coffee: The Drink That Sped Up the World

The Secret of a Nice Cup of Tea

Raising a Glass to Toast

What Is the Connection Between Marmalade
and a Sick Queen?

The Full English Breakfast

"The Name's Benedict, Eggs Benedict"

The Eggs That Were Broken to Make the
First Spanish Omelet

Eggs Florentine and the Wicked Italian Queen Who
Loved Spinach

The Noble Story of French Toast

Who Was the First Person to Pronounce on Porridge?

Canned Ham

The Surreal History of Breakfast Cereal

How Did the Croissant Get Its Shape?

My wife and I tried two or three times in the last forty years to have breakfast together, but it was so disagreeable we had to stop.

WINSTON CHURCHILL

To eat well in England, you should have breakfast three times a day.

W. SOMERSET MAUGHAM

Coffee: The Drink That Sped Up the World

It's thought that the word **coffee** may derive from the Arabic *kahwa*, a type of wine, which in turn derives from a word meaning "to have no appetite"—appropriate when you think how the day's first cup of coffee often takes the place of breakfast. This galvanizing drink is believed to have originated nearly twelve hundred years ago in Ethiopia, in the region of Kaffa—which has also been suggested as an alternative derivation of the word. According to legend, a shepherd guarding his flock noticed how jumpy his sheep became after eating the red berries that had fallen off a nearby bush. When he sampled some himself, he was amazed to feel a similar surge in energy. Word got around and soon the monks at a nearby monastery were gathering the fruit for themselves and, after many attempts, ended up with a murky brown beverage that they came to rely on to keep them awake for their nightly prayers. But it wasn't until much later, in the thirteenth century, that coffee became a truly palatable drink: it was the Arabs who discovered that roasting coffee beans, grinding them, and steeping the grounds in boiling water produced the best flavor, and the world has been hooked ever since.

ESPRESSO: COFFEE IN THE AGE OF STEAM

Throughout the nineteenth century, the era of industrialization when steam power was all the rage, people tried brewing coffee using hot water vapor. Indeed, a steam-brewing contraption at the 1896 World's Fair is said to have made three thousand cups per hour. Unfortunately, steam-brewed coffee tastes awful, since coffee needs to be made at just below boiling for it to be at its best. The first coffee machine to use steam to force hot water through very finely ground beans—a much more acceptable method—was invented by Frenchman Louis Bernard Rabaut back in 1822, but it took almost another eighty years to really catch on, and it was the Italians rather than the French who popularized it. Espresso means "fast," so it's a little ironic that it took such a long time. It wasn't until 1901, when the definitive machine was designed by Italian inventor Luigi Bezzera, that **espresso** became a café staple, speeding up life for everybody.

CAPPUCCINO: PUTTING A TONSURE ON YOUR CUPPA?

Contrary to popular opinion, this type of coffee, with its distinctive layer of frothy milk, is not named after the coffee bean used, but another group of coffee-obsessed clerics—the Capuchins. Originally part of the Franciscan order of monks in Italy, they broke away in 1520 out of a desire to get back to basics and return to the life of solitude and prayer formerly practiced by their founder, St. Francis. But the religious authorities took a dim view of this, and the heretic monks were forced into hiding. They were given refuge by the Camaldolese monks, however, and to show their appreciation began to wear the hooded *cappucio* cloaks favored by that order. The hood also helped them to stay out of trouble, serving as useful camouflage by allowing them to blend in with their hosts. Eventually the new order became respectable in the eyes of the Church, so much so that a sister order of nuns was also formed and they all settled together in Naples in 1538.

It was there, legend has it, that the Capuchins developed

the method of making their morning coffee by steaming goat's milk and pouring the froth over a mug of cold coffee drawn from a barrel. They had discovered that the foam acted as insulation and heated up the liquid beneath as they sipped it on those cold monastic mornings. **Cappuccino** means "little Capuchin," either after their coffee-brown robes or because the white foamy top of a cappuccino with its ring of brown resembles the monks' traditional tonsure—shaven on top of the head with a ring of hair around the edge.

There is a counterstory that it was a Capuchin monk, Marco d'Aviano (1631–99), who came up with the first cappuccino—directly after the Battle of Vienna in 1683 (obviously a key event for breakfast inventors: see also the story of the CROISSANT). As spiritual adviser to the Holy Roman Emperor Leopold I, he would certainly have needed a reviving cuppa after all those hours spent on his knees, praying for victory. But as the first time such a claim was made was during the celebration of the battle's tricentenary in 1983 by the Austrian press, this should perhaps be taken with a grain of salt (if not a teaspoon of sugar).

As with all monastic orders, the Capuchins' numbers have dwindled drastically over the centuries, but, to this day, the group, who also gave their name to a monkey and a squirrel, still have around six active houses in Britain, twelve in Ireland, and approximately two hundred missionary stations across the world. Perhaps they should have stuck to coffee making, as Starbucks has over twenty-five thousand of their own outlets around the globe from which an estimated 7.5 million cappuccinos are sold every single day. Now, that should cheer up the Capuchins, don't you think?

Why to Thank Café Society for Paris Hilton

Café, a small, unpretentious restaurant or coffeehouse, comes from the French word for coffee. For centuries the so-called beautiful people, or society's elite, have gathered in fashionable cafés in London, Paris, New York, Vienna, Milan, and any other city where the bright, artistic, and influential folk lived. At the end of World War I, those who had survived reconvened their regular gatherings, some of them idling the entire weekend away in the corner of a popular café. During the 1920s, American journalist Lucius Beebe (1902–66) famously chronicled their antics for the *New York Herald Tribune* in his weekly column This New York, describing them as "the Café Society."

Members were not necessarily part of the ruling classes or the Establishment, but they were closely associated, vacationed together, and attended each other's private parties. With the rise of photojournalism, many who were photographed leaving top nightspots or lunches became famous simply for being famous, leading to the ridiculous celebrity culture we have in modern times. Although the term "jet set" replaced the Café Society during the 1950s, we can still thank the original Café Society for the Kardashians and Paris Hilton.

The Secret of a Nice Cup of Tea

Tea is the most commonly consumed hot beverage in the world. The original tea leaf was cultivated from the *Camellia sinensis* bush, in Yunnan Province, China, where humans first came up with the idea that eating the leaves or boiling them in water might be enjoyable.

One early legend, dating back to the Tang Dynasty nearly five thousand years ago, claims that it was Bodhidharma, the founder of Chan Buddhism, who discovered tea. According to the story, he fell asleep while meditating one morning and stayed asleep for nine whole years. When he finally woke up, he immediately cut off his eyelids to punish himself for such idleness. He then cast them away, where they took root in the soil and grew into tea bushes.

In case that puts you off tea forever, there is another, less disturbing, legend that tells of Shennong, Emperor of China, who was drinking boiled water when leaves from a nearby tree flew into his bowl, changing its color to an amber brown. Sipping the brew, the emperor was pleasantly surprised, and so the cup of tea was born.

Tea became fashionable in Britain with the arrival of Catherine of Braganza (1638–1705), the Portuguese princess who married Charles II in 1662. When she moved into the king's court, she introduced her favorite drink, which soon became popular with the nobility and the wealthy classes of England. About that time, the first advertisements for tea appeared in London newspapers and tea began arriving in Britain by the shipload. Tea drinking became even more popular when Queen Anne (1665–1714) chose tea over ale as her regular breakfast drink. By 1750, it had become the principal drink of all the social classes in Britain, even though it was very expensive, a pound of the cheapest tea costing about one-third of a skilled worker's weekly wage.

There are two ways in which the British managed to make the cup of tea their own. The first was through their unusual preference for adding milk. In the seventeenth and eighteenth centuries, the china cups tea was served in were so delicate, they often cracked when boiling tea was poured straight into them. Milk was therefore added to cool the liquid and stop the cups from cracking. At first a necessity, this soon became a preference and is the reason why, even today, many people add milk to their cups before pouring in the tea. The second was through the invention of **afternoon tea**. Legend has it that in the 1840s Anna, 7th Duchess of Bedford—one of Queen Victoria's ladies-in-waiting—came up with the idea of a late afternoon meal to overcome the "sinking feeling" she felt during the long gap between lunch and dinner. At a time when men were traditionally out of the house, either drinking at their club, hunting, or—if middle class or below—actually doing some work, this became a very feminine ritual, celebrated with special china tea services and daintily presented cakes and SANDWICHES, and providing an amazing forum for uninterrupted gossip. By 1880, tea was a huge event. People would dress up for the occasion, and afternoon tea dances, often accompanied by a live orchestra, became extremely popular.

Tea was so important that it had even kicked off a war when disgruntled American settlers threw tons of the stuff into the sea at Boston following the decision by the British government to impose a very high tax on it. The settlers objected to having to pay tax to the rulers of a far-off land rather than to their own elected representatives. Indeed, they were furious enough to start a war over it, and what became known as the Boston Tea Party led to the Revolutionary War (1775–83), eventual independence, and America's emergence as the leading economic power in the world. I should probably point out here that that is the real reason for the Boston Tea Party and not, as I told a group of Japanese tourists the last time I was in Boston, because a Mr. Starbucks and a Mr. Nescafé got together and tossed all that tea into the harbor.

WHO WAS EARL GREY?

There are four classifications of tea: green and white, both unfermented; oolong, which is semi-fermented; and black, which is fully fermented. From these basic varieties thousands of different blends are produced worldwide. The most popular form of black tea has not only a very unusual taste but a rather strange name, **Earl Grey**.

Charles Grey, the 2nd Earl Grey (1764–1845), was prime minister between 1830 and 1834, a significant time in British politics. Despite strong opposition to his policies by the previous prime minister, the Duke of Wellington (see BEEF WEL-LINGTON), the first announcement Earl Grey made on replacing the Iron Duke (as he was known) was a pledge to carry out wide-ranging parliamentary reform that included allowing one out of every six men (from a population of 14 million) to actually vote. Previously it had been nearer to only one in twenty.

During his short time as prime minister, Grey also earned the distinction of abolishing slavery throughout the British Empire, but it was his removal of the East India Company's complete monopoly on trade with China in 1834 that led to his immortalization. This opened up the tea trade routes and ushered in the era of the tea clipper, ships packed with just that one product, such was its boom in popularity. In China the tea export business was suddenly hugely profitable, and a grateful Chinese ambassador presented the prime minister with an entirely new blend of tea that included distinctive oil extracted from the rind of the bergamot orange. As a further compliment to the earl, a cup of Earl Grey also has a grayer tone than ordinary tea.

Raising a Glass to Toast

In the beginning there was bread—which was revolutionized by the ancient Egyptians around six thousand years ago when they realized that if they let the dough sit around in the warm sunshine, it would become naturally leavened by the yeast spores in the air and once baked, it would retain its risen shape. Shortly afterward there was **toast**—when, after a few days in the dry desert air, the bread became hard and unpleasant to eat. Toasting it was a means of making stale bread edible again. The Romans spread the idea of toast throughout Europe. The word "toast" comes from the Latin *tostus*, meaning "scorched" or "burned." Toast is essentially burned bread, so the name makes sense. "Tost" was a great favorite in the Middle Ages when "sops" of bread were used to soak up wine or sweet liquids and then toasted against the heat of an open fire (see also FRENCH TOAST and MELBA TOAST).

But what is the connection between a slice of cooked bread and raising your wineglass and toasting someone? We need to look back once again to the Romans, who had a strange practice of adding a small chunk of burned bread (toast) to each glass. Some historians have suggested that this was to add flavor to the wine or to give each guest a small "treat"— like a crouton in soup. A more likely reason is that it was to remove impurities and improve the flavor of poor wines. Burned toast was like a crude form of the "activated charcoal" used in modern-day water filters to do the same job of absorbing impurities and enhancing flavor.

The habit of quaffing wines from a glass with a piece of

toast in it persisted and by the sixteenth century "drinking a toast" became the same as saying "drinking a glass of wine with a chunk of toast at the bottom." The term "toast" then stretched to the act of drinking itself, regardless of whether there was any toast in your glass, and then to the entire ceremony and even the person being honored by it. Drinking a toast became all the rage in the seventeenth and eighteenth centuries: the precursor of today's drinking games. Everyone in the room would be separately toasted and it was impolite not to drink to each of them in turn. When the party ran out of physical attendees to toast, they would then raise a glass to absent friends and then all manner of absurdly unattainable ambitions, simply as an excuse to keep drinking.

What Is the Connection Between Marmalade and a Sick Queen?

There is an old story that the word **marmalade** derives from *Marie malade* ("ill Mary," in French), referring to how Mary, Queen of Scots (1542–87), used it to settle her stomach during a bout of seasickness when sailing from France to Scotland. Yet the word was already in use well before Mary's time—first appearing in the English language in 1480, according to the *Oxford English Dictionary*. A simple linguistic confusion may be responsible for its association with a seafaring queen: the word *mar* means "sea" in Spanish, close to *mer* in French, while *malade* does indeed mean "sick" in that language, hence the connection between seasickness and Queen Mary. But, long before she was vomiting up her state banquet into the English Channel, *marmelada* was the Portuguese name for a sweet quince paste (quince is *marmelo* in that language) that was imported as a luxury to Britain from the late Middle Ages onward. So expensive that it was only used by royalty and the well heeled, *marmelada* was nonetheless in great demand. Tudor cooks invented a more affordable version by boiling up the cheaper imports of lemons and bitter Seville oranges into thick, solid conserves they called "marmalades," which were cut into slices and eaten as sweets.

When marmalade changed from a sweet into a jam is hard to pinpoint, but evidence suggests its having happened in money-conscious Scotland. In the eighteenth century, Scottish recipes included a much higher proportion of water (possibly spearheaded by a Mrs. Janet Keiller, the founder of Keiller's marmalade, in the 1790s) and changed marmalade from an expensive Portuguese dessert into a common British condiment. It was also a clever way of making sure that expensive ingredients were stretched as far as possible by spreading it on a piece of TOAST. That way the sensation of eating a chunk of Tudor marmalade was preserved at a fraction of the price and became a breakfast staple that spread around the world.

During the Middle Ages, pork was one of the few types of meat that was widely available and affordable throughout rural England. Indeed, for many, it was the only meat they ever had to eat. **Bacon** wasn't just the most delicious way to eat it: the smoked and salting process it went through meant that, unlike pork, it didn't need to be eaten immediately, and a side of bacon could keep a hungry family fed (just a small piece of bacon could make PEASE PUDDING taste much better) for a whole winter.

From this it's easy to see how **bringing home the bacon**, as the expression goes, would have been quite an event and acquiring a pig for the family pot a much sought-after prize. Catching a greased pig, one possible origin of the phrase, was popular at country fairs up and down the land: men would chase the animal around a ring, and the winner, who finally caught and held on to the pig, was then given it to take home.

A rather more likely explanation for the phrase originates from a traditional event known as the Dunmow Flitch Trials. Established by a noblewoman called Juga in 1104, this was a challenge to all married couples in England to live for a year and a day in complete harmony, without so much as a cross word between them. The prize offered was a flitch of bacon (a whole side), but, and this doesn't surprise me, in over five hundred years there were only eight winners. The tradition was reestablished in 1855, and nowadays the trials are held every four years, often with celebrities taking part, probably in aid of some fashionable charity or another. Claimants of the flitch are required to stand in front of a jury of twelve (six maidens and six bachelors) and prove their worthiness during a daylong family event. The winners "take home the bacon." Or they do in theory: these days, it would seem, conjugal harmony is just as rare as it ever was.

The Full English Breakfast

The British breakfast, I swear on my honor as a scholar, is without a peer on this globe's crust. I mean, of course, the kind of breakfast that was de rigueur when I was a student of Oxon in the balmy days before the world wars had done their worst . . . It was a parade of the ultimate subtleties in meats and fish and fruits. It weighted a man naturally towards poetry and philosophy. It broadened him out, not only in girth, but in the circumference of friendliness.

ROBERT P. TRISTRAM COFFIN (October 1948)

For a meal that has become world famous, strangely little is known about the evolution of the English breakfast. Until the mid-seventeenth century, most people would have had two substantial daily meals: lunch (known as "dinner"—see page xiii) in the late morning and supper in the early evening. Breakfast was not recognized as a meal and was only recommended to children, the sick, and the elderly, who were advised to eat small meals at regular intervals. But as lunch moved to later in the day, people became hungrier first thing in the morning, especially when their evening meal was relatively small. In countries where the evening meal was larger, breakfast did not become quite so important; indeed, in southern Europe it is still not a proper meal, but merely COFFEE and perhaps a piece of bread or pastry (see CROISSANT). In England and northern Europe, by contrast, the pattern has been quite different for hundreds of years. By the 1700s, breakfast in Britain was taken at around 9:00 or 10:00 a.m. and consisted of ale, bread, and beef. But, with an act of culinary genius, it was the Victorians who turned what was still essentially a snack into a full-scale meal, and so the medieval "dinner" was transformed into the **full English breakfast**, served BUFFET-style throughout the grand houses of the nation.

Why this meal then caught on so strongly around the world has a lot to do with the simultaneous rise of the middle classes and the British Empire. One division between the poor and the wealthy has historically been that the latter group was able to afford to eat as much meat as it liked. And the new Victorian middle classes felt the need to prove, or at least feel, they were on a similar social level to the grandiose upper classes. The Industrial Revolution lent a hand, leading to greater social mobility in which once humble families were now headed by captains of industry far wealthier than their noble counterparts. It was these upstart folk, with their growing country estates, who initiated the buffet breakfast, with its vast array of dishes, for their regular guests to enjoy when they rose in the morning, thus establishing the "traditional" English breakfast.

As the British Empire stretched across the world, so this habit spread with it—taken by the empire's administrators to India, South Africa, and Australia and retained in memory of an idealized mother country whose customs and traditions they were anxious to impose upon the inhabitants of those less enlightened (as they saw it) corners of the globe. They didn't want to integrate: they wanted to claim the world for Britain. Hence starting the day with an enormous meaty breakfast (especially in a hot climate to which such a meal was incredibly unsuited) became almost an act of faith.

So what should it actually consist of? Mrs. Beeton gives the following advice in her celebrated *Book of Household Management* (1861):

> The following list of hot dishes may perhaps assist our readers in knowing what to provide for the comfortable meal called breakfast. Broiled fish, such as mackerel, whiting, herrings, dried haddocks, &c.; mutton chops and rump-steaks, broiled sheep's kidneys, kidneys à la maître d'hôtel, sausages, plain rashers of bacon, bacon and poached eggs, ham and poached eggs, omelettes, plain boiled eggs, oeufs-au-plat, poached eggs on toast, muffins, toast, marmalade, butter, &c. &c.

No wonder old atlases showed the territories of the British Empire colored a dark dyspeptic pink! Scanning Mrs. Beeton's monumental list, we can spot some ingredients still on the menu today and forming the core of the modern full English: BACON and eggs, sausages, and TOAST. Later additions on the healthier side of things are: tomatoes, mushrooms, and BAKED BEANS. And then it's up to the cook to check the leftovers from the night before and decide whether to add anything else. The decline of the British Empire may well have had more to do with the fact that today we are far more likely to start our day with a bowl of CORN FLAKES (see BREAKFAST CEREAL for more on the breakfast counterrevolution) than a plate of bacon and eggs with all the trimmings, unless you are in a roadside café, where you would be chased out for asking for cereal, let alone anything as effete as a muffin.

One of the most enjoyable things about the full English is that no two breakfasts are the same. There are different regional variations, and Scotland, Wales, and Northern Ireland, not to mention southern Ireland, all have their own versions.

FULL SCOTTISH BREAKFAST

A **full Scottish breakfast**, along with the usual eggs, bacon, and sausage, has black pudding (ingredients: blood, pork rind, and barley), HAGGIS, and potato scones. It may also include white pudding (basically black pudding without the blood) and oatcakes. Another favorite ingredient is square sausage—a kind of sausage burger—also known as Lorne sausage.

FULL WELSH BREAKFAST

The unusual ingredient in the **traditional Welsh breakfast**—otherwise identical to the full English—is laverbread, a purée of boiled reddish seaweed that is then mixed with oatmeal, formed into patties, and fried in bacon fat. It's been eaten in Wales since the Middle Ages.

ULSTER FRY

Northern Ireland's **Ulster fry** makes a full English look positively healthy. It has seven key ingredients: BACON, eggs, sausages, farl soda bread (a triangular-shaped flat bread, split in half and fried), potato bread, black pudding, and tomatoes, all fried together, preferably in one large pan.

THE IRISH BREAKFAST

I should disclose at this point that there is, of course, a **full Irish breakfast**, one that my friends in Dublin claim was the very first and that the English stole from them. But we know that during the eighteenth and nineteenth centuries, the English were, by and large, landowners while the Irish, in general, worked on that land and were always complaining of being hungry. And we know it was the great potato famine of 1845 that drove millions of the Irish to North America (see "How the Potato Killed a Million People," page 110), so it's somewhat unlikely they were enjoying many full Irish breakfasts prior to then. Therefore, with respect to fine Irish chefs around the world who insist the English stole their breakfast, I'm afraid I can't endorse that claim.

"The Name's Benedict, Eggs Benedict"

The world's favorite brunch dish, **eggs Benedict** comprises an English muffin cut in two, each half topped with ham, a poached egg, and a dollop of HOLLANDAISE SAUCE. A number of Benedicts claim to have invented it. In 1942, the *New Yorker* published an interview with one Lemuel Benedict, a retired New York stockbroker, who told the story of his breakfast one day at the Waldorf Hotel back in 1894. Unimpressed by the menu and with a thumping hangover, he asked for "buttered toast, poached eggs, crispy bacon, and a hooker of hollandaise." According to Benedict, the maître d,' Oscar Tschirky (see also THOUSAND ISLAND DRESSING and WALDORF SALAD), was so taken with the dish that he immediately included it on the hotel menu, replacing the TOAST with a muffin and the BACON with ham.

But this is disputed by a letter sent to the *New York Times* in September 1967 by Edward P. Montgomery, who suggested the dish was in fact the idea of Commodore E. C. Benedict, a yachtsman and retired banker, who died at the age of 86 in 1920. Montgomery insisted he had the original recipe, which he included in his letter, saying it had been given to his uncle, a close friend of Benedict. Publication of this letter prompted another one, from Mabel C. Butler of Massachusetts, in which she claimed that the "true story" behind the original recipe was "well known to the relations of Mrs. Le Grand Benedict," of whom she was one. According to Mabel Butler, when the Benedicts lived in New York City, at the turn of the century, their habit was to dine regularly at Delmonico's Restaurant. One morning Mrs. Benedict complained that the menu had become too familiar and suggested more variety. As she was a regular customer, the head chef asked the good lady what she had in mind, to which she replied: "I would like poached eggs on toasted English muffins with a thin slice of ham, hollandaise sauce, and a truffle on top."

Each tale was firmly believed by its narrator, but it is equally likely that all three were referring to a dish that had been around for a lot longer, probably going by a different name. What is certain is that printed recipes for eggs Benedict were beginning to appear from the turn of the twentieth century. In *Eggs, and How to Use Them*, published in 1898 and subtitled (clearly with Mrs. Benedict in mind) "A Guide for the Preparation of Eggs in Over Five Hundred Different Styles," the reader is encouraged to "split and toast some small muffins; put on each a nice round slice of broiled ham, and on the ham the poached egg; pour over some creamy Hollandaise sauce." Meanwhile, in 1900, the *Connecticut Magazine* printed a similar recipe, suggesting readers should "Broil a thin slice of cold-boiled ham . . . toast a slice of bread, butter it, and moisten with a little water; lay the ham on it and on that a poached egg."

However, it turns out that this all-American dish could well have been European in origin. Elizabeth David, in *French Provincial Cooking* (1960), refers to a traditional French dish called *oeufs à la bénédictine* and consisting of puréed fish and potatoes on fried bread with a poached egg on top. So maybe eggs Benedict was originally a sort of full French breakfast enjoyed by Benedictine monks on days when they were forbidden to eat meat? (They'd have been eating a FULL ENGLISH otherwise, given half a chance.)

These days there are many variations on the theme, including EGGS FLORENTINE (the ham substituted by spinach), **seafood Benedict** (the ham replaced with crab, lobster, or shrimp), and **waffle Benedict** (with a waffle instead of the muffin and plenty of maple syrup in addition to the hollandaise). **Eggs Benedict Arnold**, in which the muffin is replaced by a biscuit and the hollandaise sauce with gravy, is very curiously named for such a staunchly American dish. Benedict Arnold was a general during the Revolutionary War of 1775–83 who famously switched sides and fought for the British. One of the most hated figures in U.S. history, his name has since become a byword for treason.

One of life's most perplexing questions is **What came first, the chicken or the egg?** It troubled the great Greek philosopher Aristotle (384–322 BC), who said: "If there has been a first man, he must have been born without father or mother—which is repugnant to nature. For there could not have been a first egg to give a beginning to birds, or there should have been a first bird which gave a beginning to eggs, because a bird comes from an egg." The Bible comes down firmly on the side of the chicken, describing, in Genesis 1:21, how on the fifth day of Creation God made "every winged fowl after their kind." Scientists, meanwhile, have looked at evolution and concluded that the egg came first. And to the obvious question of "Well, what laid it then?" the answer is "Not a chicken." It was a bird, though, the ancestor of the chicken, the Red Junglefowl (*Gallus Gallus*), a tropical member of the pheasant family from India and the Far East. As fossil evidence confirms, wild fowl lived alongside dinosaurs (who also hatched from eggs) and other prehistoric species, so it doesn't take a great leap of imagination to conclude that the Red Junglefowl could have crossbred with another ancient species (the Grey Junglefowl has been suggested) to produce the new breed now used all over the world for its meat and eggs. The offspring of this union would have been the first chicken—after it had pecked its way out of the egg, of course.

The Eggs That Were Broken to Make
the First Spanish Omelet

Known in Spain as *tortilla de patatas* (round potato cake), a **Spanish omelet** is made up of fried potatoes mixed with beaten eggs and sometimes onion. Using basic ingredients that were easy to forage, the dish was historically popular with soldiers on the move. Indeed, legend has it that it was created by one particular soldier, the Carlist general Tómas de Zumalacárregui y de Imaz (1788–1835).

Carlism—a political movement in support of the Infante Carlos of Spain (1788–1855), regarded by traditional royalists as the rightful male heir to the Spanish throne—was the cause of a series of civil wars in Spain during the nineteenth century and beyond. In the first Carlist uprising following the death of King Ferdinand VII in 1833, and the disputed accession of his infant daughter Isabella, Zumalacárregui took command of the troops supporting Don Carlos and, through a series of successful battles, gained possession of much of the country supporting Isabella. During the Siege of Bilbao in 1835, which resulted in the death of the doughty commander and the failure of the uprising, it is said that Zumalacárregui happened upon a remote farmhouse and demanded food from the farmer's wife. All the terrified woman had at her disposal was a potato, some eggs, and an onion, which she cooked together and served to the general. According to the story, Zumalacárregui was so pleased with the resultant dish that he ordered his army chefs to make it regularly for the entire force, and so the Spanish omelet was born.

The word "omelet" is of course French rather than Spanish, and has been used since the middle of the sixteenth century, probably modified from the Latin word *lamella*, meaning a small thin plate. The first printed reference to the word in English was in Randle Cotgrave's *Dictionary of the French and English Tongues*, published in 1611. This includes an entry for "Homelette . . . an Omelet, or Pancake of eggs." Meanwhile, *Le Pâtissier françois* (1653) by French master chef François Pierre de la Varenne—author of three groundbreaking books that form the basis of modern French cuisine (see also "From Fine Sauces to Haute Cuisine," page 139)—lists several omelet recipes; it is thought the translation of the book into English in 1660 led to the dish becoming popular in Britain. The expression **You can't make an omelet without breaking a few eggs** is a common idiom used to indicate how sacrifices have to be made in order to achieve anything of any use or importance. A sentiment General de Zumalacárregui y de Imaz would surely have agreed with.

Eggs Florentine and the Wicked Italian Queen Who Loved Spinach

The adjective *Florentine* simply means "in the manner of the city of Florence." Applied to food, it refers to something cooked on a bed of spinach—such as **veal florentine** or, most typically, **eggs florentine** (see also EGGS BENEDICT). As a noun, *florentine*, in a culinary context, originally meant a kind of pie, either savory or sweet, such as the Bedfordshire

apple florentine, an apple pie made with the unusual addition of ale and formerly a Christmas treat.

Cooking spinach in the Florentine style can be traced back to one Florentine in particular, someone who had a huge effect on the culture of Renaissance Europe. Catherine de Médicis was born in Florence in 1519. Both her parents died within weeks of her birth (her father from syphilis and possibly her mother, too, infected by her husband), but her lonely childhood only made Catherine stronger. She came from a powerful family, favored by the Pope, yet the Médicis weren't quite royalty—they had clawed their way into power through ability and sheer ambition. And Catherine was no exception. Aged only fourteen, she married Henri, the dauphin of France, and when his father, François I, died in 1547, she became Queen of France.

Her marriage was an unhappy one, however, as Henri preferred his mistress, Diane de Poitiers, heaping favors upon her and condemning his wife to a life of virtual seclusion. As a result, Catherine didn't become truly powerful until thirteen years later, following Henri's death, when she took over as regent on behalf of their ten-year-old son, François. When he died in 1560, she ruled on behalf of their second son, Charles, and then in 1574 on behalf of their last-born, Henri. Catherine was a fighter and she almost outlived them all, as Henri was murdered less than a year after her own death in 1589. She was notorious for her political maneuvering and for her persecution of the Protestant Huguenots, whom she had formerly supported, in particular for authorizing the St. Bartholomew's Day Massacre of 1572, in which thousands of Huguenots were either butchered or forced into exile abroad (see HOLLANDAISE SAUCE and MORNAY SAUCE). Huguenot writers later accused her of adopting the cynical tactics of Machiavelli (1469–1527), another hugely influential Florentine, to fell all her enemies at one blow.

Nostalgic for Italy, Catherine longed for a taste of her home town and so imported chefs from Florence. Known as "Madame Serpent" for her tendency to dispatch wayward courtiers with a dose of poison, she no doubt felt safer with members of her own retinue in charge of the royal kitchens. But she also made many innovations—she is credited with introducing table etiquette and the fork to France, for instance (see also "From Fine Sauces to Haute Cuisine," page 139)— and among the various Italian dishes produced by her chefs was a way of cooking her favorite vegetable, spinach, which so caught on that it became known as spinach *à la florentine* and then just *florentine*, spinach being implicit. The aura of sophistication and exoticism surrounding the word clearly attracted later cooks, who would apply "florentine" (minus the spinach) to any special celebratory pie, recalling as they did a city that had produced such cultured and talented, if wicked, individuals—and no doubt recognizing that every good dish needs a touch of something sinful.

The Noble Story of French Toast

What we call **French toast** is known as *pain perdu* ("lost bread") in France itself. Like TOAST, it is regarded as a way of using stale (or "lost") bread, slices of which are softened by being dipped in a mixture of egg, milk, and sugar before being fried in butter. In Britain, it was actually referred to as **German toast** until World War I when anti-German sentiment caused the name to be changed. In a similar vein, the British royal family changed its surname from Saxe-Coburg-Gotha to Windsor (see SALISBURY STEAK) and the German shepherd dog became known as an Alsatian at around the same time. In a further, somewhat ironic twist, French toast briefly became known as **freedom toast** following French disapproval of the invasion of Iraq in 2003 (see also FRENCH FRIES).

The actual German name for the dish is *arme Ritter* or "poor knights," echoing its much older English name, **Poor Knights of Windsor**. The original Poor Knights were veterans of the Battle of Crécy in 1346, one of the most important battles of the Hundred Years" War (1337–1453). Although the English won the battle, thanks to the introduction of the fearsome longbow, many knights were still captured and held for ransom by the retreating French. Forced to sell their grand estates to raise the money, twenty-six noble knights eventually returned to England alive and free but penniless. King Edward III (1312–77) then provided the veterans with a pension and accommodation at Windsor Castle and they became known as the Alms Knights, or the Poor Knights of Windsor, establishing a centuries-long tradition.

At one point, during the 1830s, the Poor Knights objected to their name—perhaps because by then they were much more affluent, they no longer appreciated sharing a name with stale, sugary, egg-soaked bread—and King William IV (1765–1837) officially changed their title to the Military Knights of Windsor. It's perhaps the association between the Poor Knights and the French that has led to the modern name for the dish.

Who Was the First Person to Pronounce on Porridge?

If I asked you to visualize the earliest scene from the history of **porridge**, I imagine you'd picture a peasant stirring a big pot on a chilly morning and not the Buddha (566–486 BC) fasting in sun-soaked India. But the making and eating of porridge is in fact central to his story. In his search for enlightenment, the Buddha did without food for so long that he fainted and a peasant girl brought him back from the brink of death with a little milk and a bowl of rice porridge. Thanks to the young girl's ministrations, he was soon strong enough to take his seat under the Bodhi Tree, where he finally achieved enlightenment.

In his teachings, first collected orally and then written down by his followers, the Buddha went on to explain the five benefits of porridge. As it turns out, these five benefits are somewhat less than transcendental and already long acknowledged by porridge eaters (Buddhist or otherwise) the world over: namely that it improves digestion, quenches thirst, suppresses hunger, and reduces constipation and flatulence. And anything that does that can only be a good thing. (For more on the Buddha and food, see page 194.)

Canned Ham

To "devil," according to the *Oxford English Dictionary*, is a culinary term for "cooking something with fiery hot spices. The term was presumably adopted because of the association between the devil and excessive heat in Hell." The practice of deviling food is an old one: James Boswell (1740–95), the famous diarist and Dr. Johnson's official biographer, frequently noted a passion for "deviled bones" for his supper.

Presumably that was a dish of spicy spare ribs rather than anything more sinister.

In 1868, a food distributor based in Boston, the William Underwood Company—a major supplier to Union troops during the Civil War (1861–65)—began experimenting by mixing ground ham with hot spices, including mustard and cayenne pepper. They christened this process "deviling" (preparing ham in this way was an innovation, even if the word itself was much older) and their product, **Underwood Deviled Ham**, soon found its way all over America, thanks largely to the canning process (see CHICKEN KIEV) and the growing rail networks. Their famous red devil logo was trademarked in 1870, the oldest food trademark in America, and the canned ham remains popular to this day.

The Surreal History of Breakfast Cereal

The brightly colored cereal boxes on your breakfast table, full of chocolate and sugar and covered in cartoon elves and grinning tigers, are in fact the unlikely last remnants of a bizarre, long-running battle that raged in nineteenth-century America between an equally unlikely set of combatants: vegetarians, water-cure fanatics, and the Seventh-day Adventist Church.

It was all powered by a growing obsession with regulating bodily functions. At the time, most Americans ate a FULL ENGLISH BREAKFAST—a substantial meal, heavy on pork and other meats and very low in fiber. As a consequence, many were very constipated and suffered painful gastric disorders.

But, being the nineteenth century, nothing was done in haste. The first spokesman in the health-food revolution was the Reverend Sylvester Graham (1794–1851). A vegetarian with no medical training, he was determined that *whole wheat* flour was the answer, and his very profitable **Graham bread** and **Graham crackers** followed as a result. Vegetarianism and temperance became wildly popular for a while: meat-eating was declared to be unhealthy—not to mention productive of equally negative carnal desires—and coffee and tea were condemned as poisons. It wasn't long before Graham's supporters were declaring that their search for "healthy" substitutes based on grains and cereals was for the common good, some no doubt recognizing how this might earn them very healthy sums of money in the process.

In 1858, Dr. James Caleb Jackson (1811–95) took over an unsuccessful water-cure resort in New York, renaming it "Our Home Hygenic Institute." Patients were subjected to a punishing regime of baths and unpleasant treatments and fed a restricted diet based on various grains, like farm animals. In 1863, Jackson created the first **breakfast cereal**, which he called **Granula**, but it was hardly fast food; it had to be soaked overnight in milk before it was even possible to chew the stone-hard crumbs. Even so, Granula caught on, earning Jackson ten times the amount of cash he had invested in developing it.

In Battle Creek, Michigan, the Seventh-day Adventists ran a health institute, the Battle Creek Sanitarium, where the latest in dietary reform was practiced, but it didn't really catch on until John Harvey Kellogg was put in charge. Dr. Kellogg (1852–1943) had been hand-picked for the job, and his medical and spiritual training had been supervised at every stage by the Adventists. Following his experience of living in a boarding house during training, where cooking was impossible and restricted to the vegetarian diet required by his religion, the hungry young man recognized the need for a ready-cooked breakfast cereal that required no preparation. In 1880, he came up with a mixture of wheat, oat, and corn meal baked in little biscuits, which he cheekily called

Granola, and it became a huge success, in the land of overnight successes.

A few years later, in 1893, a Denver lawyer named Henry D. Perky (1843–1906) invented a completely different product to cure his indigestion that he called **Shredded Wheat**. The wheat was steamed until thoroughly softened, then rolled between grooved rollers to form strands that were then pressed together and cut into biscuits, referred to by Perky as "my little whole wheat mattresses." Unfortunately, the process didn't work and the moist wheat biscuits quickly perished. Kellogg then went to see the disillusioned inventor and offered Perky $100,000 for the patents he had taken out for manufacturing his cereal, but then he lost his nerve and retracted the offer. He would later regret this, however, particularly since in his conversation he had shared his secret of how Kellogg products were dried by slow heating so that they remained in perfect condition for a long period of time. Armed with this knowledge, Perky tinkered with his machinery, began to dry his Shredded Wheat, and sat back to watch the dollars roll in, becoming immensely rich in the process.

Kellogg was naturally envious and, after a long period of experimentation, came up with a process in which wheat was cooked, flattened into flakes, and then dried. **Granose Flakes**, as he called them, would soon prove to be a significant commercial discovery, but not for the good doctor. With no real head for business, he was mostly interested in his sanatorium and for a while his patients were the only people who could buy his products.

The man primarily responsible for speeding breakfast cereal out into the grocery stores of the nation was Charles William Post (1854–1914). He entered the cereal business after a string of entrepreneurial failures that led to a physical collapse. As a patient at Kellogg's sanatorium in 1891, he didn't find a cure, but he did come to realize that health foods and, in particular, coffee substitutes were potential gold-mines. The idea alone must have been enough to cheer him up a bit. After leaving the sanatorium, he started his own health institute in Battle Creek and within four years he had developed Postum, a wheat- and molasses-based hot drink. Using everything he knew about sales, Post then mounted an advertising campaign and his product became a success.

There was, he said, no limit to the number of physical and moral ills (even divorce or juvenile delinquency) that were caused by coffee, but it could all be banished with Postum, the beverage that promised to "make red blood." Two years later, he launched what would prove to be an even bigger hit. **Grape Nuts** had been a failure as a grain beverage, as it was originally marketed, but rebranded as a breakfast cereal, it quickly became a bestseller. (It was sweetened with maltose, which Post called grape sugar and which he thought had a nutlike flavor—hence the name.) By 1902, Post was making over a million dollars a year—a lot of money now, but a huge sum in those days.

J. H. Kellogg's younger brother and general office assistant at the sanatorium, Willie Keith (1860–1951), followed with an improvement on the Granose idea—flakes made from corn. Eventually, the two Kellogg brothers parted ways and in 1906, W. K. (whose signature still appears on every cereal box as the company's trademark today) founded the great Kellogg breakfast food empire with his toasted **Corn Flakes**. Originally called the Battle Creek Toasted Corn Flake Company, it was renamed the Kellogg Company in 1922, while the product on which it was founded became what must be the most celebrated breakfast cereal in the world. At the time of its conception, hundreds of other would-be cereal pioneers had leapt into the field as well, many journeying to Battle Creek itself to start their businesses. Soon thirty different cereal flake companies, most of them fly-by-night operations, had crowded into the small town. And Americans had scores of cereals to choose from, each promising to cure their every ailment.

But despite their origins in the health-food movement, breakfast cereals have no special nutritional value, beyond the food value of the grain they are made from—hence the fact that so many today are artificially "fortified" with extra vitamins. It is the milk they are eaten with that provides most of the nutrients they otherwise lack.

How Did the Croissant Get Its Shape?

The **croissant**, cornerstone of the "continental" breakfast the world over, first came about during the late 1830s, when August Zang, an Austrian artillery officer, founded a Viennese Bakery at 92 rue de Richelieu in Paris. Zang's shop sold all kinds of Viennese delicacies, including the **kipferl**, a crescent-shaped pastry common in Austria since at least the thirteenth century. His kipferl was so popular that bakers all over Paris rushed to make their own French version, and the croissant (meaning "crescent") was born.

There are all kinds of culinary legends explaining the unusual shape of the kipferl and hence croissant, mostly connected to the fact that the symbol of Turkey, and thus Islam, is a crescent moon. One story says it was invented in Germany to celebrate the Muslim defeat at the Battle of Tours in

732; others suggest that it dates from the Crusades. But my favorite is that it celebrates the failure of the Turkish siege of Vienna in 1683 (see also CAPPUCCINO), when bakers, up in the middle of the night to prepare their bread for baking, heard the Turks digging a tunnel under the city walls and quickly raised the alarm. The Turks, taken by surprise, were soundly beaten. The crescent-shaped pastry the bakers then made to mark the Turkish defeat allowed the Viennese to relive their victory every time they tore one in half or dipped it into a cup of coffee. But whichever story is the true one, and however the croissant acquired its distinctive shape, it remains a fact that the definitive French pastry is not French in origin but Austrian.

2
Lunchbox

Did a Satanist Really Invent the Sandwich?

Who Invented the Picnic?

Ship's Biscuit: When Did a Snack Take the
Place of Lunch?

Whatever You Do, Don't Mention the
Quiche (Lorraine)

Ask not what you can do for your country. Ask what's for lunch.

ORSON WELLES

Did a Satanist Really Invent the Sandwich?

Sandwich is, believe it or not, not really even a proper word. It is a proper name, however. The village of Sandwich, first recorded in AD 642, is a picturesque and historic place in southeast England: its name evolved from the Old English words *sand* and *wic*, meaning "Sand Village" or "Town on the Sand." Now two miles from the sea, it was once a thriving seaport—the first captive elephant landed there in 1255, before being delivered as a gift to Henry III—and the home of King Charles II's naval fleet under the command of Sir Edward Montague. When in 1660 his grateful king made Montague an earl, the latter pondered which of the great ports he would honor with his new title. Bristol was one option and Portsmouth another, but the naval commander settled for Sandwich, and so his hereditary title became the Earl of Sandwich.

To date there have been eleven earls, but the most famous of them, the one who provided the key ingredient for every packed lunch in the Western world, was number four. John Montague (1718–92) was, like his great-grandfather, First Lord of the Admiralty, but unlike him, he was both corrupt and incompetent. The navy was in a state of complete disarray by the time it was called into action during the Revolutionary War (1775–83): the eventual defeat of the British forces was regarded by many as his fault. And hardly surprising, as the earl was far more interested in his life outside work, particularly gambling. Indeed, it was this that gave rise to the great culinary legend forever associated with him. According to the famous story, he was once playing cards long into the wee small hours in 1762 with friends. Drunk and on a winning streak, Sandwich decided he needed some food and ordered waiters to bring him some meat but "between two slices of bread." This was to prevent his fingers from becoming greasy and marking the cards, helping his opponents to figure out his gaming pattern. The strategy worked, and the snack soon caught on at the great gaming tables and gambling clubs of England, the "sandwich" quickly becoming part of the English way of life.

It didn't help his reputation that Sandwich was also a member of the notorious Hellfire Club, a gentlemen's society set up to ridicule organized religion. No one knew what went on at their meetings—members didn't discuss them—but rumors were rife of orgies and satanic rituals. It was reputedly at one of these meetings that he became the victim of one of history's great one-liner putdowns. Sandwich is said to have abused Samuel Foote: "Sir, I don't know if you will die on the gallows or of the pox." To which Foote shot back: "That, my lord, depends on whether I embrace your principles or your mistress." The story was speedily spread around London by his many enemies.

By his death in 1792, Sandwich had become the most unpopular man in England. Even friends suggested his epitaph should read: "Seldom has any man held so many offices and yet accomplished so little." Yet the sandwich is not his only legacy to history. As First Lord of the Admiralty, Sandwich was one of the sponsors of the voyage Captain James Cook made to the New World in 1778. On January 14, Cook became the first European to visit the Hawaiian Islands, which he originally called the Sandwich Islands in honor of his benefactor. Although the islands changed their name a century later, the South Sandwich Islands and the Sandwich Straits still bear the name of the old gambler, and inventor of the sandwich, to this day. Not to mention the expression it has given rise to, in the sense that we can now find ourselves *sandwiched* between two objects or two business appointments or, as I would much prefer, between two cocktail waitresses in a Las Vegas casino. I'm just relieved that the first earl selected Sandwich for his title. I'm not sure I'd fancy a cheese and CHUTNEY bristol, or a ham and tomato portsmouth. Would you?

WHAT ABOUT THE OPEN-FACED SANDWICH?

The **open-faced sandwich**, particularly favored in Nordic countries (see SMORGASBORD) and consisting of a single slice of bread with food items arranged on top, is a much older concept than the double-slice variety. It goes back to the Middle Ages, when a large chunk of bread called a "trencher" was used as a plate to hold other food. At the end of the meal, the bread could be eaten or, if the diner had had enough, left on the floor for the dogs to devour.

AND WHY IS IT A CLUB SANDWICH?

A **club sandwich**, also known as a **clubhouse sandwich**, has its origins in America. Usually made with three slices of bread, this double-decker sandwich traditionally consists of BACON, chicken, lettuce, and tomato, always on toasted bread. The sandwich was apparently made famous by the exclusive Saratoga Springs gaming club in New York during the late 1800s, when it became a firm favorite on the menu. Ever since the Americans had added MAYONNAISE and all sorts of sauces to the common sandwich, greasy fingers were evidently once again a problem for card players, which the toasted version helped to solve.

Who Invented the Picnic?

At the end of the eighteenth century, a new fashion crossed the English Channel. The French were having a new type of informal party, known as a *pique-nique*, in which the guests would bring along a share of the food and wine so that the burden of providing would not be left to only one family. Consequently, these social get-togethers were often held in outdoor public places, and to this day **picnic** is used to describe an outdoor meal, usually with friends.

It has been suggested that the word "pique" might derive from one of the senses of the French verb *piquer*, "to pick," while "nique" is something "irrelevant" or "of no importance." This is just speculation, however, as according to the *Oxford English Dictionary*, the origin of the word isn't known. It was first used in English during the mid-eighteenth century, associated initially with poker playing and later to describe a meal of cold foods eaten outside during a hunt—a tradition dating back to the mid-1300s and usually involving game pies and roasted or baked meats.

When the great royal parks of Paris were opened to the public for the first time, following the Revolution in 1793, *pique-nique* culture took off with a vengeance and Londoners who were used to looking to Paris for the latest fashions in clothes and culture promptly set up their own version, the

"Picnic Society," whose members would each arrive with their share of the overall feast. The nationwide enjoyment of picnicking was firmly established in England by the mid-1800s, and many of the great writers of that era and later, including Charles Dickens, helped to popularize the custom in their fiction.

Ship's Biscuit: When Did a Snack Take the Place of Lunch?

Now, luckily for you, this is not something you'd recognize as a lunchtime dish. But in the past when sea voyages could last months or even years and with a decided lack of storage space for fresh food aboard ship, this unappetizing dried bread formed the major part of a sailor's daily ration. When Richard the Lionheart set off on the Third Crusade in 1190, he loaded his ships with an early form of **ship's biscuit**, which he called "biskit of muslin." By the time of the Spanish Armada (1588), a sailor's daily ration was one pound of biscuit and one gallon of beer. Sailors gave it all kinds of nicknames, from "hard tack" ("tack" was their word for food) to "sheet iron" and "tooth dullers." Ship's biscuit was made edible only by being dipped in a liquid or some kind of gravy.

The *Encyclopedia Britannica* of 1773 notes: "Sea biscuit is a type of bread much dried by passing the oven twice to make it keep well for sea service. For long voyages they bake it four times and do so six months before embarkation and it will hold good for a whole year."

Made from the cheapest flour (the captain's and officers' rations were from finer), ship's biscuit was notorious for supplying an unintended source of protein: weevils and maggots. It certainly explains why sailors traditionally ran riot and drank themselves blind as soon as they got off their ships. They were probably trying to block out the memory of months of gnawing on maggoty ship's biscuit.

Whatever You Do, Don't Mention the Quiche (Lorraine)

World War II ended over sixty years ago, but the Germans remained very unpopular in France for many years. After D-Day (June 6, 1944), the French punished any kind of fraternization with the occupying enemy extremely sternly, and there was a wave of executions without trial, public humiliations, assaults, and detentions of suspected collaborators—all of which makes the real history of their most popular lunchtime dish a tad embarrassing for them, which is exactly why I am telling it.

Located in the northeast of the country and now firmly French, Lorraine has always been the subject of territorial disputes, and over the last couple of hundred years has been occupied by both the Prussians and the Germans on many an occasion. Lorraine's very name is Germanic, coming from Lothringen, a German kingdom of the Middle Ages, but this doesn't often come up in polite conversation with its pro-French inhabitants. During World War II, the fight to drive the German army out of France was so intense that General de Gaulle chose the Cross of Lorraine as the symbol of the French Resistance. Consequently, Lorraine is now host to the largest American military cemetery in Europe. And yet the region has long been strongly influenced by the culture and cuisine of its German neighbors, as is shown by its most famous export, **quiche Lorraine**. Its pastry was originally baked in the same cast-iron tin as German custard tarts—indeed the filling, made with eggs and milk or cream, is a type of savory custard. The word "quiche" actually derives from the German word *Kuchen* for "cake" or "tart," later mangled into *Kische* and then *quiche* by the French. Thus the most famous French dish in the world is actually a garbled version of the German phrase the "cake of Lothringen."

Although the recipe for quiche was first developed as a simple meal to cater for people on religious fasting days when abstinence from meat was essential, the key ingredient of Lorraine's quiche is BACON. A favorite staple of Allied soldiers fighting on the Lorraine battlefields, who brought the recipe back home with them in the late 1940s, it has been available in just about every supermarket in Britain and America ever since.

3
Fast Food

A hot dog at the ballgame beats roast beef at the Ritz.

HUMPHREY BOGART

A Quick History of Fast Food

Fast food goes hand in hand with urban living—people lacking the space or time to prepare food for themselves—and as the Romans are credited with the invention of the town, so it is most likely they who first came up with the idea. In Roman cities much of the poorer population were packed into *insulae* ("islands" in Latin), multistory apartments built out of cheap materials—proving that high-rise accommodation is not such a new concept either. With little opportunity to cook for themselves without burning down the neighborhood, many had to depend on food vendors for their meals. This wasn't what we would recognize today as fast food—in the mornings, bread soaked in wine was eaten as a quick snack, and cooked vegetables and stews were in demand later in the day—but the idea behind it is the same.

By the Middle Ages, all large towns and urban areas supported numerous vendors, providing a huge range of dishes. As in the cities of antiquity, these establishments catered for those without cooking facilities: workers, the poor, travelers, and pilgrims. At a time when the daily diet of most people living in the British countryside consisted of simple fare such as PEASE PUDDING, the food on offer would have seemed highly sophisticated: the pilgrims in Chaucer's *Canterbury Tales* (1387–1400), for instance, are constantly talking about snacks, and munch their way through everything, from pasties and roasted onions to desserts such as blancmange (vanilla pudding).

This kind of food fascinated people living in rural areas,

who had a much more limited and unimaginative diet. Even quite lowly folk in the cities had access to a huge variety of speedy meals: then as now, it was all part of the instant gratification of urban life. These precursors of the burger bars and fried-chicken outlets that litter (quite literally) today's inner cities had only their owners' voices and distinctive jingles to make them stand out from the crowd. As a consequence, London became notorious for the constant racket from vendors trying to drown each other out.

The modern version of the hawker's cry is, of course, the advertising jingle, but the intention is just the same—to get us to part with our money for an alluring snack or ready-cooked meal, which these days can be popped in the microwave and heated in the blink of an eye.

FAST FOOD TAKES OVER AMERICA

A hundred years ago, on July 7, 1912, a fast food restaurant called the Automat opened in New York. The Automat was a revolutionary cafeteria with ready-prepared foods on sale behind hinged windows, which the customer then purchased by inserting coins in a machine. This really was instant gratification and it wasn't the first of its kind—its owners, Joseph Horn and Frank Hardart, had set up their first in Philadelphia in 1902—but New York's Automat created a sensation. The demand was so great that huge lines snaked back down Broadway and in fact it could take rather longer to get your food than in a conventional restaurant, but its fans didn't care: food had finally moved into the twentieth century. Numerous Automat restaurants were built all around the country to deal with the demand. The company also popularized the notion of **takeout food**, with their slogan "Less Work for Mother," although the idea wasn't a novel one: German immigrants had been preparing and selling their cooked sausages (see HOT DOG) for half a century by then. Soon another concept altogether became popular and the Automat was relegated to a mere footnote in the history of fast food. And that concept was the HAMBURGER restaurant.

Two brothers from New Hampshire, Dick and Mac McDonald, opened a BARBECUE drive-in in 1940 in San Bernardino, California, and after discovering that most of their profits came from hamburgers, the brothers reopened their restaurant in 1948 as a stand offering a simple menu of hamburgers, FRENCH FRIES, milkshakes, and Coca-Cola, all served in disposable cartons. The McDonalds wouldn't have seen it like this, as, in their eyes, their approach was ultra-modern, but by drastically simplifying their menu, they were going back to the model of the medieval food vendors who had concentrated on one key product they excelled at. As a result, the brothers were able to produce hamburgers and fries constantly, without waiting for customer orders, and could serve them immediately; and their hamburgers were only 15 cents, about half the price they would have cost at a typical diner.

The transformation of the McDonalds' hamburgers into a global phenomenon wasn't down to the brothers, however, but to ferocious businessman Ray Kroc, who had originally specialized in milkshakes. Kroc bought the brothers out in 1954 (later refusing to pay the royalties that had been verbally agreed at the time) and then introduced two things that were to make McDonald's a world leader: production lines inspired by Henry Ford's car factories that meant the food was perpetually being replenished; and a ruthlessly maintained policy of standardization that ensured that every branch would serve exactly the same food in exactly the same way. It was so successful that all other fast food chains promptly followed suit and American fast food proceeded to take over the world.

A **bistro** is a FAST FOOD café, or at least it was until ultra-fast food outlets began to dominate in the 1970s. After the defeat of Napoleon at the Battle of Waterloo in 1815, troops from all over Europe began to occupy Paris, particularly the Russians. Naturally the French cafés were soon bustling with new visitors, trade was roaring and one of the most frequent shouts to be heard at the time was "*Bweestra! Bweestra!*," which means "Quickly! Quickly!" in Russian. Hence the word soon became associated with cheap bars, small clubs, and cafés.

The Hamburger: From German Snack to American Icon

The **hamburger** is commonly acknowledged as America's signature dish, and it's estimated that Americans eat over 14 billion of them every year. So you can see how being the home of the hamburger could mean big business, and this is indeed the claim of the small town of Seymour, Wisconsin. Seymour's Hamburger Hall of Fame celebrates the history of burgers, while the town's annual one-day Burgerfest includes parades and competitive events themed on burger-related condiments, including the famous Ketchup Slide. In 1989, the world's largest hamburger was produced during the festival, weighing in at a queasy 5,500 pounds. Back in 1885, as the town informs its visitors, fifteen-year-old Charles Nagreen was selling minced-meat patties from his stall at the very first Seymour Fair. Hamburger Charlie, as he became known, soon worked out that his meatballs weren't selling because customers weren't able to easily walk around eating them. So

Charlie flattened his meatballs, served them between two slices of bread, and named them hamburgers after the hamburger steaks that were already popular in the northern states.

Charlie Nagreen continued to sell hamburgers at county fairs for the rest of his life and became a local celebrity, claiming right up to his death to be the inventor of this form of FAST FOOD. But there is a rival claim, also dating from 1885. According to this story, sausage-making brothers Frank and Charles Menches were accidentally sent beef instead of pork by their supplier. Short of time and with limited resources, they decided to cook up the beef instead and serve it in sandwiches at the Erie County Fair, naming their new concoction the hamburger sandwich after their home town of Hamburg in the state of New York.

And there are all kinds of other counterclaims: no less an institution than the Library of Congress has credited Louis' Lunch, a restaurant in New Haven, Connecticut, with making America's first burger in 1895. But eminent hamburger historians (and yes, they *do* exist) have begged to differ, citing instead Old Dave's Hamburger Stand at the 1904 World's Fair in St. Louis, run by Fletcher Davies, a restaurant owner from Athens in Texas. So convincing was their argument, in fact, that the Texas State Legislature then confirmed Athens as the "Original Home of the Hamburger" in November 2006.

While they argue it out among themselves, let us take a look instead at the northern Europeans, who have been eating minced, salted, and preserved steak ever since Genghis Khan hacked his way around the continent during the early 1300s (see STEAK TARTARE). Nineteenth-century German immigrants used ships of the Hamburg America Line, which began crossing in 1847. The immigrants took their favorite recipes with them and their easily prepared fast food of minced meat and bread was soon in demand along all the busy ports of the East Coast. Incoming passengers on the Hamburg Line, referred to as Hamburgers, called their favorite snack of ground meat served in a round bun a *Brötchen* ("roll" in German), although these were soon being called hamburgers by New Yorkers after the travelers who were eating them. We know this because by the mid-nineteenth century (well before any of the "official" claims), food vendors along New York Harbor were advertising "steak cooked in the Hamburg style" to attract newly arrived German passengers and crew. As early as 1802 the *Oxford English Dictionary* had been defining **Hamburg steak** as a type of salted beef.

On reflection, it is fair to suggest that, with the rapid spread of the Hamburg steak throughout America, one man alone is unlikely to have come up with the notion of slipping meat into a bun. After all, back in England and rather earlier, in 1762, John Montague had had the same idea himself (see SANDWICH), and the British aristocracy has never been known for its inventiveness. It's true that, as America expanded and the rail and road networks granted travelers easier access over greater distances, so the food-on-the-move industry exploded into life (see FAST FOOD). Yet the famous meat-filled bun that fueled that expansion can most likely be traced not to a single American but to a host of northern European migrants leaving the port of Hamburg for the Brave New World.

Salisbury Steak: The Food Fad That Rescued the Hamburger from the Enemy

Basically a HAMBURGER without a bun, the **Salisbury steak** was the invention of one eccentric man, the Dr. Atkins of the nineteenth century: Dr. J. H. Salisbury (1823–1905). A trained doctor and chemist, Salisbury joined up as an army medic when the Civil War broke out in 1861. After some time, he noticed that the main medical problem for soldiers in the field was not bullets but diarrhea—due, in his view, to a poor diet (although I'd have put my money on anxiety in the face of the enemy as the most likely cause). Salisbury believed that a healthy diet was directly responsible for a healthy body. These days, of course, all of us are aware of how important our diet is for health, but back in 1861 this was radical thinking. Salisbury's conclusions were treated with suspicion to begin with until it soon became evident that the regular intake of minced steak, onions, and coffee he recommended led to a huge improvement in the health of the rank and file (or perhaps they'd just gotten over their battle fright by then).

Salisbury also believed (somewhat less sensibly) that vegetables and starchy foods could produce substances in the digestive system that poison and paralyze the tissues, leading to heart disease, tumors, tuberculosis, and mental illness. He maintained that our teeth were principally "meat teeth" and our digestive systems designed to digest lean meat, hence fruits and vegetables, fats, and starches should make up only a third of our diet. Starch was digested slowly, so it would ferment in the stomach and produce vinegar, acid, alcohol, and yeast, all of which were harmful to our systems. The cult of Salisbury flourished and by 1888 he was prescribing his special recipe, now called Salisbury steak, to be eaten three times a day, together with lots of hot water to rinse out the digestive system, as a "meat cure" for rheumatism, gout, colitis, and anemia.

But if it weren't for the outbreak of World War I, it is unlikely that the Salisbury steak would be well known today. During the war, most English-speaking nations began renaming anything that sounded remotely German, to the extent that the British royal family changed its surname and

America's favorite dish, the hamburger steak, instead became known as Salisbury steak among the Allied forces, the term subsequently spreading throughout the English-speaking world.

Not to mince your words is to speak plainly, frankly, and with brutal honesty. The phrase is always used in the negative sense, as in "not to"—we never hear anybody complaining of someone "mincing their words," after all (we're clearly all amenable to a spot of flattery or economizing with the truth). The first recorded use of the expression can be traced to Joseph Hall's *Cases of Conscience* (1649), making it one of our older sayings. Some things we are told are unpleasant and difficult to take in and perhaps need to be made more "digestible"— hence the analogy with butchers mincing cheaper cuts of meat, often full of bones and gristle, to make them easier to swallow. It has always been felt that a person "not mincing his/her words" is making no effort to soften their impact.

From Swords to Skewers:
The Rise of the Kebab

Legend has it that the **kebab** was born over the open fires of medieval Turkish soldiers, who impaled meat on their swords and then grilled it. References to skewers of grilled meat go back far further, however: ancient Greeks from Homer to Aristophanes wrote about an earlier variant of the kebab, the *obeliskos* (meaning "little spit," it's also the origin of the word "obelisk," a narrow thin monument such as the Washington Monument). Yet the dish was old even then. After all, when you think about it, the cooking of meat over a fire must date back to approximately the day after prehistoric man first discovered how to light one.

However, while most of our culinary techniques, such as roasting, toasting, and baking, are centuries old, grilling meat kebab-style was largely unknown in Western Europe until around thirty years ago. That is because the nature of the dish reflects the differences in cuisine and lifestyle between West and East. In Europe, where the weather is cooler, it would have been easier to store whole joints of meat for roasting. In the Near East, by contrast, where before refrigeration the hotter temperatures would have meant meat spoiled much faster (the Jewish prohibition of pork and shellfish began as an entirely sensible rule for a tribe of desert-dwelling nomads), smaller cuts would have been more practical. In addition, fuel has long been in short supply in the hotter, drier Near East, with fewer trees to chop down for firewood, but used to be superabundant in Europe. Traditional European cookery therefore comprises methods that use much more fuel, such as baking and roasting, while Near Eastern cuisine has concentrated on much quicker methods, such as grilling and frying.

The word "kebab" has an interesting history, deriving from *kababba*, an ancient Arabic word, meaning fried—not grilled—meat. A fourteenth-century Arabic dictionary describes a *kabab* as a dish of fried chunks of meat with some liquid. The Arabic word for grilled meat, by contrast, was *shiwa*. The Turks then took both words and combined them into the **shish kebab**, in which the liquid element of the *kabab* has been transmuted into a marinade that renders the meat more succulent and stops it from drying out when it is cooked over an open fire.

Now the term has become central to Arabic culture and cuisine. In Persian poetry, *jeegar kabab kardan*, meaning to break somebody's heart, translates literally as "to grill liver," while in Iran the word for "kitchen" used to be *kabab khaneh*, literally "grill house" or "kebab house."

WHERE DOES THE DONER KEBAB COME FROM?

Kebabs come in many different forms, but the shish and doner kebabs are the best-known varieties. The drunker a kebab-shop's customer, the more likely he is to order a **doner kebab**. Translated as "rotating roast," its origins lie in the expansion of the Ottoman Empire into Europe and their picking up the European habit, when roasting larger joints of meat over a fire, to slice cooked strips off the outside of the joint, allowing the raw meat underneath to take its turn. Descendants of the Ottomans running modern kebab restaurants all over Europe slow-roast their meat in just this way.

The idea behind roasting the meat vertically, in what is known fondly by fans everywhere as "an elephant's leg," is a modern method of self-basting, dating from the nineteenth century. It is intended to coat and infuse the roasting meat with dripping fat for a longer period than horizontally roasted meat. The grayish meat of an average doner kebab is undoubtedly of poor quality, but the suggestion that its name refers to the notorious Donner Party of 1846 (led by George Donner), where starving pioneers snowbound in the Sierra Nevada resorted to cannibalism, is just a scurrilous rumor. Likewise nobody has recorded how or why the word "kabab" evolved into "kebab" throughout modern Europe, but presumably it's because, after eight beers and at two in the morning, it's marginally easier to say.

How Eating Fish and Chips Became a Religious Experience for the British

Until the middle of the sixteenth century, eating meat on a Friday was an offense punishable by hanging, and so led directly to the national habit of eating **fish and chips** on that day.

The law originated with the Christian tradition that believers must abstain from eating meat on a Friday. Jesus Christ was executed on Good Friday and for hundreds of years Christians have honored his sacrifice and atoned for their sins by denying themselves meat on that day of the week. Luckily for hungry Christians everywhere, the Church, like many supposed vegetarians, doesn't regard fish as meat, so that is why you now see huge lines outside fish-and-chip shops all over England every Friday, although I doubt many realize that, by not eating meat, they are honoring or atoning for anything.

There has long been a link between fish and Christianity. Not only were some of the Apostles fishermen but, back in the days when conversion to Christianity was punishable by death, the secret sign for the religion was a simple drawing of a fish: the Greek word for "fish" was also an acrostic that spelled out "Jesus Christ, God's Son and Savior." There is a more pragmatic story that the Church invented the rule purely to boost fish sales, but sadly there is no evidence to back it up.

Fish fried in batter was originally a Jewish dish, one that became increasingly popular in the East End of London where many Jews settled during the early nineteenth century. Charles Dickens refers to a fried fish warehouse in *Oliver Twist* (1839), and Henry Mayhew, in his epic four-volume survey of London (1851–62), estimated there to be already around three hundred fried-fish sellers in the city.

Fried chipped potatoes (see also FRENCH FRIES) go back further, probably dating from the late eighteenth century, and chip sellers were traditionally Irish (see "How the Potato Killed a Million People," page 110, for more on Ireland's dependence on this vegetable). Previously the most popular form of potato-based FAST FOOD had been the BAKED POTATO, but in the nineteenth century the taste for chips spread, particularly in Scotland and the north of England: they became a complete craze in the mill towns of Lancashire. Interestingly enough, it was Dickens once more who was the first to call this snack "chips" in print: the *Oxford English Dictionary* cites his description in *A Tale of Two Cities* (1859) of "husky chips of potatoes, fried with some reluctant drops of oil."

A wave of chip shops spread down from the north and a wave of fried-fish shops spread up from the south until eventually the two overlapped. In 1860, a Jewish immigrant named Joseph Malin opened a shop, on Cleveland Street in the East End of London, selling fried fish "in the Jewish fashion" alongside fried chipped potatoes for the first time. Demand was so great for this new, cheap "fast food" that Malin soon opened fish-and-chip shops all over London.

But it was the arrival of the steam-powered fishing trawlers in 1877 that really revolutionized the industry, allowing owners of fish-and-chip shops to buy cheaper fish in much greater quantities. By the end of the century, fish-and-chip shops were as much a part of British culture as steam trains and working-class poverty. By 1925, there were thirty-five thousand shops, accounting for two-thirds of all the fish caught around the British Isles. Essayist and general expert on British poverty George Orwell rated fish and chips first among the home comforts in his book *The Road to Wigan Pier* (1937), going as far as to say that the dish had "averted revolution" (and perhaps inventing the concept of "comfort food" in the process).

The government was clearly paying attention, for, during World War II, fish and chips were judged so important to the national morale in Britain that they were one of the few foods to avoid rationing (helped by the fact that they didn't need to import either fish or potatoes). Although enthusiasm for Indian, Italian, and Chinese cuisine (see chapters 10–12) has led to a reduction in the number of old-fashioned fish and chips restaurants, there are still nearly nine thousand left in Great Britain. And that is over seven times the number of McDonald's restaurants (see HAMBURGER). Fish and chips now accounts for 20 percent of all takeout meals bought on a Friday, and it's estimated that in excess of 250 million fish-and-chip suppers are eaten throughout the UK every year, which makes them something of a national institution. Now, that is something worth celebrating.

The Sausages Whose Bark Is
Worse Than Their Bite

The **hot dog** feels like a very modern snack, and under that name it does indeed date back only to the twentieth century. But under its alternative name of **frankfurter** it has a much longer pedigree.

Immigrants from Germany brought their favorite sausage to America with them: one that they had been eating since the Middle Ages. Indeed, Frankfurt celebrated the frankfurter's five hundredth birthday in 1987. By 1564, when Maximilian II was crowned Holy Roman Emperor, the snack was sufficiently established for it to be given out to the people of Frankfurt in celebration. The association between "sausage" and "dog" is more recent, however, dating back to the early nineteenth century when a talented Frankfurt butcher, Johann Georg Lahner (1772–1845), created a new recipe that gave his sausages such a distinctive smooth brown appearance that he called them "dachshunds" or "little dogs." (That also works in reverse, of course: as dachshunds look so very much like frankfurters, perhaps that's how they acquired their nickname of "hot dogs.")

But it was only after it moved to America that the frankfurter really came into its own. As the Germans settled all over the country, they introduced their favorite dishes to their new neighbors, and the frankfurter became extremely popular. There are claims from all over the United States as to who was the first to put it into a roll, including at least two versions of an unlikely story that the original frankfurter vendors lent their customers white gloves to eat the hot sausages with, to stop them burning themselves, but as customers kept walking away with them, they decided to offer them bread instead. While it may be open to debate who actually came up with the idea of putting sausages into rolls, there is little doubt about how the frankfurter hit the big time and who was behind it. When Christian von der Ahe (1851–1913), another canny German, bought the St. Louis Brown Stockings baseball team in 1882, one of his first ideas was to set the ticket price at just 25 cents, ensuring full crowds who would consequently spend much more money on his beer and frankfurters, a move leading to the birth of the long association between the sport of baseball and hot dogs, one that endures to this day.

The term "hot dog" is popularly believed to have been coined during a baseball game, in fact, between the New York Yankees and the Giants in 1901. It was a chilly day and concessionaire Harry Stevens decided to buy up all the dachshund sausages he could find, his vendors offering them for sale with the following cry: "They're red hot! Get your dachshund sausages while they're red hot!" Observing the vendors, newspaper cartoonist T. A. Dorgan sketched a dachshund dog inside an elongated roll and, apparently unable to spell "dachshund," used the caption "hot dog" instead, a term that quickly caught on.

Dorgan wasn't the first person to play around with the notion of an actual dog in a bun, as attested by this satirical poem that appeared in a Yale student rag six years before:

> 'Tis dog's delight to bark and bite,
> Thus does the adage run,
> But I delight to bite the dog
> When placed inside a bun.

This reflected the suspicion at the time that the best cuts of meat weren't always finding their way into the cheap sausages, which, for all one knew, might actually contain dog meat. Whatever they contained, hot dogs clearly didn't taste too bad, as consumption of them never let up. Manufacturers of frankfurters initially tried to avoid the term, but with anti-German sentiment running high during World War II (see also FRENCH TOAST and SALISBURY STEAK), "frankfurter" was dropped in favor of "hot dog"* and, under this name, quickly rose to become the American icon it is today.

French Fries: What Did the Belgians Ever Do for Us?

French fries represent the perfect balance between the Old and the New World. America supplied the potato, imported in the sixteenth century by Spanish explorers. The earliest specimens, like the tomato (see GAZPACHO), were initially used medicinally, in small quantities, as an ingredient in pills, salves, and therapeutic potions. But then Europe supplied the perfect cooking method. Belgian historians have found evidence that inhabitants of the Meuse Valley near Liège were cutting potatoes into strips and frying them as long ago as 1680. The French love their *pommes frites*, but even they admit the recipe is Belgian in origin. And then America reimported the recipe, and the favorite side dish was born.

But so why aren't they called Belgian fries? One story goes that the French fry was given its name by American GIs stationed in Belgium at the end of World War II. Thinly cut crispy chips garnished with MAYONNAISE are a Belgian speciality they would have been able to buy from any street corner. Apparently this delicacy was then incorrectly named "French" because the bemused GIs thought that, as the Belgians were speaking French, they must be in France.

However, the real story goes back rather further, originat-

---

*During World War I, dachshunds (the actual dogs, that is) had been renamed "liberty pups."

ing with Thomas Jefferson (1743–1826). Long before the days of being branded as cheese-eating surrender monkeys, France had a very close relationship with the United States. They had helped in the Revolutionary War against the British, and Jefferson then spent five happy years, between 1784 and 1789, as ambassador to France. During that time Jefferson grew to love its culture and cuisine and encouraged his servants to study French ways. As a result, the ambassador returned to America with a wide range of ideas that he was eager to introduce to the New World.

When he became president in 1801, he hired a French chef, Honoré Julien, to work at the White House, and his resulting banquets were reported in great detail to a fascinated public. At one of them Jefferson introduced a food he called "potatoes fried in the French manner," which was subsequently shortened to "French fries."

The term has been used ever since, that is until a few years ago, when the decision was made in 2003 to invade Iraq. When France objected, this led to a big dip in enthusiasm among some Americans for all things French, including various foods. Inspired by the renaming of German-sounding items that took place in Britain and America during the two world wars (see HOT DOG and SALISBURY STEAK), restaurant owners rebranded various French-sounding foods (see also FRENCH TOAST), and the favorite side was suddenly transformed into **freedom fries**.

The word **barbecue** was first used in England during the mid-1600s to describe a wooden framework for sleeping on, the term evolving over the years to mean a framework for laying out and drying fish as a means of preserving them. Just as the origin of MARMALADE has been ascribed to the French for a seasick queen, so it is tempting to assume "barbecue" must be from the French *barbe à queue* ("beard to tail"), referring to an animal being cooked whole. But sadly this is not the case. It actually derives from the Spanish *barbacoa*, adopted from the term used by the Arawak Indians of the Caribbean to refer to a wooden grill for cooking meat. Upon this framework a large animal would be roasted over an open fire.

An interesting modernization of the word exists in aerospace technology, As a spacecraft rotates to allow heat from the sun to be spread evenly over its surface, it executes what is termed the "barbecue maneuver" or is deemed to be in "barbecue mode." Although, considering the queasiness that must induce in the astronauts, I think I would have called it the DONER KEBAB maneuver or mode.

4
Aperitifs and Appetizers

Eating's Cheating: The Sickly History of the Aperitif

How Mother's Ruin Became the Sahib's Savior:
The Story of the Gin and Tonic

Shaken Not Stirred: The Martini

The Bloody Mary: Drinking to a
Brutal English Queen?

A Drink That Can Knock You Out

Waiter, There's a Mosquito in My Canapé . . .

. . . And an Outhouse in My Hors d'Oeuvre

A Crisp Riposte

Hummus: Not a Royal Dish Shocker

A Smorgasbord of Delights

Taking the Lid Off Tapas

"A dry martini," he said. "One. In a deep champagne goblet."

"Oui, monsieur."

"Three measures of Gordon's, one of vodka, half a measure of Kina Lillet. Shake it very well until it's ice-cold, then add a large thin slice of lemon peel. Got it?"

"Certainly, monsieur." The barman seemed pleased with the idea.

"Gosh, that's certainly a drink," said Leiter.

Bond laughed. "When I'm . . . er . . . concentrating," he explained, "I never have more than one drink before dinner. But I do like that one to be large and very strong and very cold and very well-made."

IAN FLEMING, *Casino Royale*

Eating's Cheating: The Sickly History of the Aperitif

Aperitif comes from the French term for an alcoholic drink that stimulates the appetite. Deriving from the Latin verb *aperire*, "to open," it was originally a medical treatment based on the doctrine of humorism, popular in medicine from classical times up until the nineteenth century. This argued that the human body is made up of four basic substances (humors) and that all illnesses are the result of an excess or deficit of one of these substances, treatable by restoring its balance within the body. So if a patient had a fever, for instance, it meant he had too much blood and needed to be bled. If he had no appetite, it needed to be stimulated with something bitter, to encourage the flow of bile and aid digestion. The medicines prescribed for this were liquors flavored with strong-tasting herbs and spices. Over time, the medicines' bitterness was dissipated by the addition of more alcohol, and then it wasn't long before the healthy also started developing a taste for them as an appetite-stimulator before a meal.

The strongly herbal taste of drinks such as Dubonnet and vermouth was deliberate: you weren't getting drunk, you were getting better—a view heartily endorsed by myself and Mr. Jameson. And drinking an aperitif soon became a social tradition in many parts of Europe, before spreading to the New World. The preferred British and American aperitifs (GIN AND TONIC and MARTINI, respectively) happily picked up on the idea of a medicinal drink before dinner, each beverage including enough strong alcohol to make sure you properly wet your whistle while whetting your appetite (see below).

The expressions **wetting your whistle** and **whetting your appetite** are often confused because they sound so similar, but they are in fact very different in meaning. One suggestion for the origin of "whistle" in "wet your whistle" is that drinkers at British pubs once had a whistle baked into the handle of their ceramic mugs. Whenever they needed more beer, they would blow the whistle to get served. I'd love to drink in a pub with such attentive service, but sadly neither it, nor this style of drinking vessel, has ever existed: "whistle" is just a joking reference to your mouth or throat and to the fact that you can't easily whistle when your mouth is dry. Whereas if you are trying to "whet your appetite," the allusion is to the sharpening of tools on a whetstone (grindstone): "to whet" simply means "to sharpen." Hence "whetting your appetite" is "sharpening your appetite." It is first referred to in Thomas Shadwell's play *The Squire of Alsatia* (1688): "Let's whett; bring some Wine. Come on; I love a Whett."

How Mother's Ruin Became the Sahib's Savior: The Story of the Gin and Tonic

Now the favorite drink of the British middle and upper classes, **gin** has a rather darker history, as its nickname "mother's ruin" suggests. Originally made in Holland in the early seventeenth century, it was popularized in Britain by the new Dutch king, William of Orange, when he took the throne in 1689. Back then, gin (its name a mangling of the Dutch *jenever*, meaning "juniper," the berries of which were used to flavor it) was at first promoted as a powerful medicine for the stomach. But people soon discovered that it offered a far quicker and cheaper way to fall over than drinking beer. And when the government allowed unlicensed gin production, thousands of gin shops, known mockingly as *gin palaces* because they were so rundown, sprang up throughout England.

It's hard to imagine now, but with no controls on gin production in those days, the drink was adulterated with turpentine—cheaper to obtain than juniper berries—and, rather than soothing the stomach, it began to have an increasingly lethal effect on its drinkers. The social degradation it caused is immortalized in William Hogarth's famous engraving *Gin Lane* (1711), which shows a London street in lecherous, drunken chaos, at its center a woman dropping the baby she is nursing. In deliberate contrast, its companion engraving, *Beer Alley*, created at the same time, is a scene of happy, boozy patriotism. By 1730, the production of gin had increased to six times that of beer and there were real concerns that gin was bringing about a complete moral collapse of Britain's working classes. Hogarth's image was used by campaigners in an attempt to get the lax laws tightened up. The Gin Act of 1736 tried imposing high taxes on the sellers of gin, but when the prices went up, there were riots in the streets. The second Gin Act, of 1751, was more successful, as it forced distillers to sell only to licensed retailers and brought gin shops under the jurisdiction of local magistrates.

London's newly regulated recipe soon became a world favorite. So much so that **London dry gin** remains the predominant variety on sale today. And as the British Empire spread across the globe, settlers took gin along with them—it was a lot less bulky than beer—as a taste of England and to blot out homesickness.

Many of these territories, especially India and East Asia, were plagued with malaria, a recurrent, frequently lethal, disease caused by mosquito bites and for which there was only one effective medicine. Back in the sixteenth century, Jesuit missionaries had observed Quechua Indians mixing the ground bark of the Peruvian cinchona or quinine tree with sweetened water to offset the bark's extremely bitter taste and then using it to treat cramps and fever. They had then imported some back to Rome, to deal with the symptoms of a particularly virulent outbreak of malaria in the early seventeenth century, which had accounted for the death of at least one pope and several cardinals. It turned out that the bark didn't just relieve the symptoms, it cured the disease, too. And from then on, anyone spending time in a malarial zone was strongly recommended to take a daily dose of quinine.

Indian tonic water (tonic meaning "cure") was devised to make that process more pleasant. The original recipe was simply a solution of quinine in carbonated water, but as it tasted extremely bitter, members of the East India Company stationed abroad started dosing their tonic water with gin, which they would then drink at sundown—the time of maximum danger from mosquitoes. Soon quaffing this new APER-ITIF had become such an integral part of their lives (they even brought it back with them to Britain) that they forgot that it had originally been just medicinal.

Shaken Not Stirred: The Martini

You ought to get out of those wet clothes and into a dry martini.

MAE WEST

The American aperitif of choice is the **martini**—a mixture of GIN and vermouth, often garnished with an olive. The inclusion of vermouth shows that the drink did at least start as something vaguely medicinal (see APERITIF): the earliest advertisement (from 1896) shows a wife plying her exhausted husband with a martini as a restorative.

It's entirely appropriate for such a strong drink that no one can remember who invented the first one or where the name came from. Americans tell the story of a friendly barman making a specially strengthened pick-me-up for a weary traveler on his way to Martinez, California. The British claim to have named the drink after the Martini-Henry rifle, notorious for kicking like a mule, which was standard army issue during the empire-building 1880s. The Italians, meanwhile, trace the name to the drinks manufacturer Martini & Rossi, which was

selling Martini Rosso vermouth from 1863. So, who knows—
any or indeed all of these may have contributed to the name.
What is certain, however, is that the first published recipe for
the martini, in Harry Johnson's *New and Improved Illustrated
Bartender's Manual* (1888), was American.

Far from being stopped by Prohibition (see CAESAR SALAD),
the martini only grew in popularity in speakeasies all over
America. The strong taste of the vermouth masked the rawness
of the homemade gin bootleggers brewed up in their bathtubs,
and by the time the laws against alcohol were repealed in 1933,
it had become the drink of choice for the sophisticated, notably
F. Scott Fitzgerald, Dorothy Parker, and most of Hollywood.

Ever since the 1930s, the martini has become increasingly
potent, the proportion of vermouth decreasing over time. At
one point it made up a third of the drink, now it's closer to a
fifth or sixth, with purists suggesting simply waving a firmly
closed bottle of vermouth over your glass of icy gin. But the
key thing remains that you have to have a strong head to
drink more than one. At the height of the Cold War when
Russia's premier Nikita Khrushchev was served a particularly potent martini, he called it "the USA's most lethal
weapon." So it's hardly surprising it was James Bond's drink
of choice, although being Bond, he had to make his own adap-
tations to the recipe (see page 64).

A **Mickey Finn** is a drink that has been drugged, usually to render a person helpless so that a crime can be
committed. (You may have heard it as "slipping a
mickey.") It is named after the owner of a sleazy Chicago
establishment, the Palm Garden Restaurant and Lone
Star Saloon, located on Whiskey Row. Taking its name
from a scruffy palm in a pot next to the reception desk,

the place was a haven for pickpockets and petty thieves, mostly trained by Finn himself. One of Finn's favorite methods was to lace drinks with chloral hydrate (knockout drops) and then fleece his unconscious victims before dumping them in the street outside. Unsurprisingly, the Palm Garden was soon closed down, in 1903, although Finn escaped jail and found work as a barman again, where he passed his techniques on to other unscrupulous vagabonds. So don't leave your drink unattended anywhere: you never know who's watching.

The Bloody Mary: Drinking to a Brutal English Queen?

Said to be the perfect hangover cure, a **Bloody Mary** is made up of vodka, tomato juice, and various strong seasonings, such as cayenne or BLACK PEPPER and Tabasco or WORCESTERSHIRE SAUCE. It is also said to have been named after the Catholic queen Mary I (1516–58), affectionately remembered as "Bloody Mary" thanks to her relentless pursuit of Protestant dissenters, of whom nearly three hundred were burned at the stake. Presumably the color of the tomato juice is thought to resemble the blood she spilled, but the drink's connection with her becomes a little tenuous when you discover that the first reference to a vodka and tomato drink called a Bloody Mary was in Paris in 1921. I doubt the French would be naming a new cocktail after an English queen; in fact, I doubt the average French barman would even know who she was. A more likely candidate in those days would have been the movie star Mary Pickford (1892–1979), after whom another red-colored cocktail had previously been named.

New York gossip columnist Lucius Beebe made one of the earliest established references to the drink in 1939 when he noted: "George Jessel's newest pick-me-up which is receiving attention from the town's paragraphers is called a Bloody Mary: half tomato juice, half vodka." Nearly three decades later, in 1964, the *New Yorker* printed a story suggesting a French chef called Fernand Petiot had invented the cocktail in all its spicy glory. The magazine quotes Petiot:

> I initiated the Bloody Mary of today. Jessel said he created it, but it was really nothing but vodka and tomato juice when I took it over. I cover the bottom of the shaker with four large dashes of salt, two of black pepper, two of cayenne pepper and a layer of Worcestershire sauce. I then add a dash of lemon juice and some cracked ice, put in two ounces of vodka and two ounces of thick tomato juice, shake, strain, and pour. We serve a hundred to a hundred and fifty Bloody Marys a day here in the King Cole Room [the fashionable cocktail lounge at the St. Regis Hotel in Midtown Manhattan] and in the other restaurants and the banquet rooms.

Other accounts back this up, suggesting it was indeed Petiot who invented the drink. And as he was working in Paris back in 1921, perhaps he was the very barman unlikely to have been acquainted with Queen Mary.

Like GIN, the Bloody Mary has also been touted as the perfect healthy breakfast. With this in mind—and strictly for the purposes of researching this book, you understand—I recently sampled twelve of these healthy breakfasts in a row at Johannesburg airport while waiting for a connecting flight, and I have this advice for you, dear reader: don't try it yourself.

The phrase **the hair of the dog** is a contraction of "the hair of the dog that bit you." Early English medical theory suggested rubbing the hair of a particular dog into the wound caused by its bite, in the belief this would heal the wound—a crude form of homeopathy, you might say, following the idea that like cures like. The phrase was used in many different contexts until settling down as a hangover remedy. These days a few more drinks the morning after a night of heavy drinking is said to cure the effects of a hangover and is known as "the hair of the dog."

A Drink That Can Knock You Out

Punch, beloved of parties and PICNICS (not to mention carolers), is a drink to be avoided at all costs. Some hosts seem to regard it as their duty to make it using the strongest alcohol available. A big mistake, as it usually ends up tasting like it should be poured into the engine of a rusty tractor. Punch feels like a British drink through and through, but it's not. During the early 1600s, as English explorers first made their way to the Indian subcontinent, one of their discoveries was a popular local drink consisting of five different ingredients: water, fruit juice, spirits, sugar, and spices. The Hindi word for five is *panch*—from the Persian *panj*, from which the English numeral "5" is also derived—and this is how the drink became known when it was served back in England at social gatherings. Unfortunately, in my experience, some people seem to delight in including paint thinner, paraffin, and white spirit, which is not the idea at all.

Waiter, There's a Mosquito in My Canapé . . .

Eaten by the French since the eighteenth century, **canapés** traditionally consist of little platforms of pastry, TOAST, or crackers with any of a whole variety of more interesting foods perched on top. Like the APERITIF, they are designed to pique the appetite. Generally salty or spicy, to encourage those holding them to drink more, and small enough to be eaten in one bite, canapés are intended to be held in one hand while, most important, the drinking hand remains free at all times. Possibly the best-known canapé is the vol-au-vent, a puff pastry case—so light that, according to the original French, it "flies in the wind"—filled with mushrooms, shrimp, or other items.

The word "canapé" has a strange history, curiously unrelated to food. In ancient Greece, a *konops* was a mosquito, while the curtains suspended around a couch to keep them out—an early form of mosquito net—were called a *konopion*. This was then adapted by the Romans as *conopeum*, becoming *canopeum* in medieval Latin and then *canope* in Middle English, as the name for a curtain, leading eventually to the modern word "canopy." The French, by contrast, used the word *canapé*—from the same linguistic root—to describe the couch rather than the curtain. Someone must have joked that a piece of toast topped with a savory food looked like a sofa (*canapé*) covered in cushions, and so the word took on the additional meaning.

. . . And an Outhouse in My Hors d'Oeuvre

Hors d'oeuvres are the grown-up version of CANAPÉS, equally elaborate but rather more substantial. By the turn of the twentieth century, the hors d'oeuvres cart had become a familiar feature of grand restaurants all over Europe. It would have been laden with all manner of colorful terrines and molds, elaborately decorated pies, salads, and tarts. Rather than reading the menu and deciding what *sounded* good, you could see which dishes actually *looked* the most appealing and try a little of several.

When first used, back in 1596, *hors d'oeuvre* (literally "outside the work" in French) was an architectural term referring to some kind of outbuilding not incorporated into an architect's main design. By the time it had been adopted into English, in the early 1700s, it had shifted in meaning to "something out of the ordinary" but fairly soon acquired its modern, food-related sense of "something outside the main meal." The expression became a familiar one in Paris at the beginning of the nineteenth century when the great chefs formerly employed by the French nobility and now liberated following the French Revolution opened their own restaurants. Hors d'oeuvres were an ideal way of displaying their culinary skill and expertise to a whole raft of new customers. While the French monopoly on fine food over the centuries can be rather annoying, there is one consolation. The next time you are served canapés or hors d'oeuvres, just remember that what it really means is that our friends across the ocean are eating sofas outside their houses.

A Crisp Riposte

On August 24, 1853, George "Speck" Crum (1822–1914) was working as head chef at Moon's Lake House in Saratoga Springs, New York, when a customer complained that his FRENCH FRIES were too thick and not "as they should be." Crum was so annoyed by this remark that he decided to exaggerate his response by slicing the potatoes as thinly as he possibly could. To his great surprise, the customer was delighted, and **Saratoga Potato Chips** proved to be so popular with other diners that Crum was soon able to open his own restaurant with the profits he made from his new recipe.

Hummus: Not a Royal Dish Shocker

Hummus, the dip made from cooked and mashed chickpeas, is very popular in the Near and Middle East. Indeed, the word means "chickpeas" in Arabic. Chickpeas have been eaten for thousands of years and were a common street dish (see FAST FOOD) in ancient Rome. (According to Plutarch, the famous Roman orator Cicero was named after an ancestor who had a wart on his nose shaped like a chickpea—which is *cicer* in Latin.) The other ingredients of hummus—sesame seeds, garlic, lemon juice, and olive oil—come from plants that have also been cultivated since ancient times. No one knows when they were first mixed together to produce the dish, but, like the KEBAB, hummus clearly goes back a long way. Thus the legend that it was first prepared in the twelfth century by Richard the Lionheart's princely enemy Saladin seems highly unlikely and a bare-faced attempt to raise the reputation of this ordinary peasant food a notch or two.

A Smorgasbord of Delights

The Swedish have been creating smorgasbords since the Middle Ages. Originally their version of HORS D'OEUVRES, a Swedish **smorgasbord** now consists of a whole variety of dishes to be eaten BUFFET-style. In Norway it is called a *koldtbord*, in Denmark they have their own version, known as a *kolde bord*, while the Finnish call theirs *voileipapoyta*. In each case, the word can be translated into English as "cold table," the exception being the Swedish term, which loosely translates as "table [*bord*] of OPEN-FACED SANDWICHES [*smörgås*]."

In Sweden back in the fourteenth century, the upper classes would serve a selection of cold appetizers—always with bread and butter—on a side table, which guests would eat standing up before sitting down to the main meal. By the seventeenth century, the food had moved from the side table to the main table and hot as well as cold dishes were served, so that what had begun as a starter now became a whole meal in itself. Today in Sweden even the grandest meals are still served in this way, including the traditional CHRISTMAS DINNER, the *julbord* (literally "Yule table").

The smorgasbord arrived in the English-speaking world at the New York World's Fair in 1939 when it was presented at the Swedish Pavilion's Three Crowns Restaurant, and soon fashionable restaurants in New York and London were offering their own versions. Now, so firmly entrenched is the word in the English language that it's not just applied to food but used figuratively to mean an array of objects, rather like the *smorgasbord* of entries in this book—please help yourself.

Taking the Lid Off Tapas

Many cultures have a rule that you must have a bite to eat every time you have a drink. Spain has taken that idea and developed a whole cuisine around it—**tapas**. Consisting of a wide range of little snacks or appetizers, from juicy olives to spicy chorizo or rings of fried squid, these are now served in select bars or restaurants throughout Spain, Britain, and the United States.

It's possible that they evolved as part of the traditional

Spanish working day, which began at first light. At 1.00 p.m., the hottest part of the day, workers would have their main meal, after which they would take a siesta somewhere shady for a few hours to allow their lunch to digest before they returned to work. From the middle of the evening until late at night, they would then socialize, drink wine, and graze on various small, easy-to-eat foods.

That's all very likely, but there is, as you might imagine, a better tale to tell. King Alfonso X (1221–84) was a very popular ruler of Castile, León, and Galicia. One day, as legend has it, he fell ill and the royal doctor advised him to take small snacks between meals in order to build up his strength. When the king eventually recovered, he continued with this regime, having decided that as eating between meals helped counteract the effects of the wine he was drinking all day, it must be beneficial for him. Reasoning that his subjects would also be drinking wine and might be consuming more than was good for them, he passed a law ruling that wine could not be served in the taverns or inns of his kingdom unless the innkeeper provided a small snack with each glass. To comply with the laws, wine would then be served with a slice of bread, cheese, or ham that a drinker could cover his tankard with to keep the flies out of his liquor. When the mug had been drained, the food was eaten and the process would start all over again, sometimes lasting all night, and so the institution that is *la tapa* was born.

The world's first tapas bar was opened in Seville in 1670, when a local nobleman bought an old convent canteen and dining room and began providing tapas, in their present form, to merchants and traders. El Rinconcillo, as the tapas bar has been known ever since it opened, was bought by ancestors of the present owners in 1860 and remains an integral part of the old city of Seville. The word *tapa* may be translated as "lid," possibly tracing its origins to King Alfonso's concern for his wine-soaked subjects, his subsequent drinking law, and the practice among Spanish workers of covering their wine with food to keep the bugs out of their drinks. Which must mean that while the French are eating their sofas (see CANAPÉS), the Spanish are dining on their lids.

Over the years, tapas have become more sophisticated, and a vast number of dishes are available. These days many people, especially if they are dining with me, try eating all sorts of food "tapas" style. The next time you are in a restaurant, and not just a Spanish one, try ordering a half dozen starters and nothing else. It's a great way to share a meal.

5
Soups and Starters

Was Bouillabaisse a Food of the Gods?

Vichyssoise: A Soup by No Other Name

Gazpacho: Together We're Stronger

Who Invented Onion Soup?

The Buffet: From Elegant Dining to
Pit-Stop Refueling

Shrimp Cocktail: The Sophisticated Snack
That's All About Saying No

Why Imam Bayildi Was a Turk's Delight

Foie Gras: How the Fig Transformed
Liver into a Delicacy

Do you have a kinder, more adaptable friend in the food world than soup? Who soothes you when you are ill? Who refuses to leave you when you are impoverished and stretches its resources to give a hearty sustenance and cheer? Who warms you in the winter and cools you in the summer? Yet who also is capable of doing honor to your richest table and impressing your most demanding guests? Soup does its loyal best, no matter what undignified conditions are imposed upon it. You don't catch steak hanging around when you're poor and sick, do you?

JUDITH MARTIN ("Miss Manners")

Was Bouillabaise a Food of the Gods?

Possibly the most famous fish soup in the world, **bouilla-baisse** is really a fish stew, a one-pot meal and the signature dish of Marseilles in the south of France. The story the Marseillais tell is that it was invented by the Roman goddess of love, Venus, who served it to her husband, Vulcan, to lull him to sleep (presumably French films hadn't been invented by then) so that she could go off and consort with Mars (the protector of the town).

Every decent chef in the world has his or her own variation: the only constant requirement is the freshness of the fish. The type of fish depends on the morning's catch, although a traditional bouillabaisse should contain at least three kinds, including the fearsome-sounding *rascasse* or scorpionfish, so called because of its arsenal of venomous spines. The name of the stew doesn't directly relate to fish but more to the process of cooking it, deriving as it does from the French verbs *bouillir* ("to boil") and *abaisser* ("lower [the heat]"). The dish was developed by Marseilles fishermen, who would put a pot of seawater on to boil by the dock, adding a few herbs and vegetables and letting it simmer over an open fire while they enjoyed a few glasses of wine in a nearby café and then, at the last moment, popped in any unsold fish, usually the small or misshapen ones.

The first recipe for bouillabaisse was published in 1790 in *La Cuisine de santé* by Jourdain Le Cointe, who called the dish *matelote de poisson* ("mariner-style fish stew") and went on to describe fishermen disembarking along a riverbank, to be met by their wives who already had a pot on for the fish to be added to. Now, that's just about as fresh as you can get.

The French have a similar dish, a slow-cooked meat stew that became popular with the meat traders at London's Smithfield Market. Like bouillabaisse, **pot au feu** (literally "pot on the fire") could be made up using any pieces of leftover or unsold merchandise, and was eaten communally. Indeed in Marseilles, its place of origin, bouillabaise is usually made for at least ten people, the idea being the bigger the stew the more varieties of fish can be included and the better the dish.

Vichyssoise: A Soup by No Other Name

Hot leek and potato soup is a staple of the winter cuisine of most north European countries, but it took a French chef, Louis Diat (see also SOLE VÉRONIQUE)—sensibly based in New York during World War I—to turn it into a classic summer dish by serving it cold and sprinkled with chopped chives. Diat, who came from the Bourbonnais, not far from the town of Vichy (hence the name of his creation), was inspired by memories of a hot soup served by his mother when he was a lad. When World War II broke out and Vichy was chosen as the new capital of Nazi-governed France, some expat French chefs tried to call the soup *crème gauloise* instead, but unlike the many German-sounding foods rechristened in the previous world war (see FRENCH TOAST and SALISBURY STEAK), this time the name, **vichyssoise**, proved indelible.

Gazpacho: Together We're Stronger

Spain seems such a straightforwardly Catholic country that it is surprising to discover that between 711 BC (when General

Tariq ibn Ziyad began his campaign to conquer the peninsula from Morocco) and AD 1492 (when Ferdinand II of Aragon defeated the last Islamic garrison at Granada) most of Spain and Portugal was Muslim. It is estimated that by the year 1200 over 5 million of the region's 7 million inhabitants were naturalized Muslims. Once the Catholics had taken over again, they were determined to stamp out over 750 years of Muslim influence and so set up the Spanish Inquisition to track down anyone continuing to practice Islam (or indeed any other religion) in secret. The Inquisition was ruthlessly efficient: between 1540 and 1700, it rounded up 104,000 so-called heretics, who were then either burned at the stake or driven from the country altogether.

This policy of zero tolerance fortunately didn't extend to Moorish architecture, and, rather than being destroyed, landmark buildings were turned either into churches (the Mezquita in Córdoba) or royal palaces (the Alhambra in Granada), even retaining their original names. But probably the strongest Moorish influence still visible in modern Spain can be seen in its cuisine, the most famous example being **gazpacho**. Made from bread, tomatoes, red peppers, garlic, and olive oil all puréed together and served cold, gazpacho is the perfect food for the dry heat and desert-like conditions of Andalucía in southern Spain. Derived from a garlic-based soup the Moors brought with them from northern Africa, the name is believed to originate from the Moorish *caspa*, meaning "residue" or "fragments," an allusion to the small pieces of bread and vegetables in the soup. But as it was made in great quantities for country laborers, who would approach the communal bowl, dip their bread in, and sit back to eat it while another took their turn, this could refer equally well to all the bits of bread that broke off and got left behind in the bowl.

However, the key ingredient of gazpacho, as we'd recognize it today, could have only been added to the recipe after the Moors had been expelled. It feels like it has always been part of our diet, but the tomato wasn't introduced into Europe until the sixteenth century—brought back from South America by Cortez in 1521—and it wasn't until the early 1600s that it was widely eaten in Spain. By adding it to the original, Moorish ingredients in the soup, the Spanish made gazpacho their own.

Who Invented Onion Soup?

The renowned expert on Mediterranean food Elizabeth David was unimpressed with the "sodden bread, strings of cheese, and half-cooked onion floating about" in a typical "French" **onion soup**. Made from caramelized onions in a beef stock and traditionally served with croutons and grated Gruyère, the soup has many imitators—some more palatable than others. But arguably the original dish is itself an imitation, as the French were by no means the first to come up with it.

Cheap, tasty, and easy to grow, onions form the basis of many types of soup the world over, and have done since ancient times. The Persians, for instance, produced their own version of a simple onion soup, thought to date to the time of King Arsaces during his military campaigns of 250 BC against the King of Syria. Onions are also the basic ingredient in Persian *âsh-e-nazri* or **pledge soup**. This is traditionally served by a family seeking support for one of its members—a sick child, for instance, or a son or daughter leaving on a long journey. The soup accompanies prayers for the child's recovery or the traveller's safe return. Other ingredients vary but are donated by relatives, friends, and neighbors in equal quantities in order that the rich are not seen to be showing off and the poor are not left feeling inferior. Everyone contributes to the making of the soup, ensuring there is enough for all and plenty left over for distribution to the hungry and homeless. If and when their prayers are answered—the child recovers or the traveler returns safely—then the soup is made every year on the same day as a ritual to give thanks to God.

Both the Persians and the ancient Greeks believed onions provided a man with courage and good fortune and their foot soldiers are known to have lived on a diet of onion soup with dried bread broken into it, beating the French to their croutons by a couple of thousand years.

The Buffet: From Elegant Dining to Pit-Stop Refueling

The word **buffet** now denotes any sort of meal in which diners serve themselves from a range of dishes, either for a starter or the whole meal. Developed in France in the eighteenth century, in a similar way to the Swedish SMORGASBORD, the food was served on long, specially made cabinets, while drawers in cupboards underneath held the plates, cutlery, and, most importantly, the wine. The practice soon spread throughout Europe, becoming popular in England in the second half of the nineteenth century.

It is said that the buffet was named after one Pierre-Alphonse Buffet (1692–1756), a Parisian gentleman, drinker, gambler, and general layabout. Like Lord SANDWICH, he also had a passion for cards and may be remembered in the same way. Because Buffet also hated to interrupt his card games with the trivial matter of eating, he ordered his servants to leave dishes on a side table so that he and his guests could help themselves to whatever they wanted whenever they chose. An alternative version of the story suggests that, having staked and lost his dining table in a game of cards, he was forced into using a side table instead, thus inventing the buffet. However, as the only reference I can find to Pierre-Alphonse Buffet is in relation to one or other version of this tale, I smell a French rat.

A buffet is indeed a type of sideboard from which food is served, but sadly there was no card-playing Monsieur Buffet (or not one connected with French cuisine), as the word derives from the Old French for "stool," *bufet* (not from the similarly pronounced *bouffer*, "to eat"). The traditional French buffet, laid out with considerable artistic and gastronomic panache, was rather smart, whereas the word has become somewhat devalued in English. No longer aristocrats gracefully grazing but stressed-out workers fighting over the last sandwich (limp and plastic-wrapped) in a cafeteria or train buffet car.

Shrimp Cocktail: The Sophisticated Snack That's All About Saying No

Archaeologists sifting through ancient middens (rubbish heaps)—see, it's not all Indiana Jones—have found evidence showing how shellfish of all kinds have been a favorite snack in coastal areas since prehistoric times. What's more, they have been eaten in a spicy sauce for at least two thousand years. Shrimp served in a spiced white wine vinegar and egg yolk sauce is an ancient Roman recipe, often attributed to Apicius, the Roman gourmet from the first century AD who wrote the earliest cookbooks. According to legend, Apicius was such a great fan of shrimp that when he heard that there were particularly large, luscious ones in Libya, he chartered a ship there on the spot. But so disappointed was he by the first ones brought to him aboard ship that he sailed home immediately, without ever setting foot on shore.

In the 1970s, all sophisticated dinner parties began with **shrimp cocktail** (moving on to BEEF WELLINGTON and CHEESECAKE). Although basically an ancient dish, the shrimp cocktail as we'd recognize it today is a much more recent creation, deriving from American recipes in the early twentieth century. Incidentally, around the English-speaking world the terms "shrimp" and "prawn" are used interchangeably, which can lead to a certain amount of confusion. "Shrimp" is used in America to describe both large and small crustaceans in the Penaeidae and Pandalidae families. The British, on the other hand, use it to describe the smaller variety (the word derives from Middle English *shrimpe*, "to contract"; hence perhaps its informal meaning of someone who is small in stature) and "prawn" to describe the larger. So the British version of the **shrimp cocktail** is the prawn cocktail.

A survey of American cookbooks confirms that shellfish in a spicy tomato-based sauce (usually ketchup mixed with HORSERADISH, Tabasco sauce, and cayenne pepper—see THOUSAND ISLAND DRESSING) and served in tiny cups as an appetizer was very popular in the early part of the twentieth century. But it was the 1920s and the decade of Prohibition that made the dish wildly fashionable. As alcohol was forbidden by law, there was a real frisson in ordering up a cocktail—even if it was just a few shrimp in a fancy glass. It was a safe way of thumbing your nose at authority. **Fruit cocktail**, likewise, was another favorite choice of the rebellious diner. (For other ways in which people coped in the era of Prohibition, see CAESAR SALAD.)

Something that **warms the cockles of your heart** induces a glow of happiness and goodwill. Could a common shellfish have any connection with the phrase? In coastal regions of the British Isles, cockles were once a staple part of the diet for many people (hence Molly Malone wheeling her wheelbarrow through Dublin's fair city, crying: "Cockles and mussels, alive, alive oh!"). As they are roughly heart-shaped, with ribbed shells, it may be that the shape and riblike veining of the heart reminded surgeons and anatomists of the cockle, but that feels rather tenuous. The more likely reason comes from the medieval Latin term for the ventricles of the heart, *cochleae cordis*. *Cochleae* sounds much like "cockle," so the phrase may well have started as a doctor's joke, deliberately mangling the Latin. *Cochlea* in Latin is actually the word for a snail; in modern anatomy it is the term used for the inner ear, due to its snail-like structure, and it's likely that the chambers of the heart used to be so called for the same reason. So if this derivation is right, we should really be speaking of warming the snails of one's heart. Which brings us, rather neatly, to that favorite starter of the French—**escargots** with garlic butter. By the way, the French are estimated to eat some twenty-five thousand tons of snails each year, equating to around 500 million snails—a statistic guaranteed to warm the heart of many a Gallic restaurateur.

Why Imam Bayildi Was a Turk's Delight

Imam bayildi—eggplant stuffed with tomato, garlic, and onion and simmered in olive oil—is one of Turkey's most popular starters. Curiously, the name has nothing to do with its ingredients but translates as "the imam fainted." One of the most important religious positions to be granted in the Arabic world is that of the imam. As leader of a mosque, the imam leads the prayer during Islamic meetings. He may also be regarded as the leader of his community. But what does a religious leader, and a fainting one at that, have to do with a Middle Eastern appetizer?

According to Turkish legend, one day, a long, long time ago, an imam, who was known for his love of food, surprised his friends and family by announcing he was to be married. The lady in question was the daughter of a well-known olive oil merchant and so, as part of her dowry, her father gave the groom twelve great jars of olive oil, each large enough to hold a fully grown man.

One day, soon after the wedding, the young bride, who turned out to be an excellent cook, presented her husband with a special dish of stuffed eggplant cooked in copious amounts of olive oil. The imam was so delighted with the dish that he asked his wife to make it every single day, which she did—until the olive oil ran out, of course. His wife then had the difficult task of informing her husband that they were out of oil and, as the tale concludes, the imam was so shocked that he fainted.

Foie Gras: How the Fig Transformed Liver into a Delicacy

A traditional French delicacy, **foie gras** (literally "fat liver") is made from the liver of a goose or duck that has been artificially fattened. The technique for producing it is thought to have been developed as long ago as 2500 BC, by the ancient Egyptians. Observing how the livers of migratory geese became enlarged due to overfeeding in preparation for their long flights, they tried force-feeding domestic birds with figs to achieve the same effect. In the tomb of Mereruka—who served as vizier, the second most powerful man in the kingdom, during the sixth dynasty—there are stone carvings of geese being force-fed, showing how the practice was already widespread by 2300 BC.

Goose fattening spread from Egypt to the Mediterranean, where the practice is recorded by Roman commentators. Pliny the Elder, for instance, describes how the gourmet Apicius (see also SHRIMP COCKTAIL) tried to apply the method to other animals, too: "Apicius made a discovery, that we might employ the same artificial method of increasing the size of the liver of a sow, as with that of the goose. It consists in cramming them with dried figs and when they are fat enough, they are drenched with wine mixed with honey, and immediately killed" (*Natural History*, AD 77–79).

The Romans called the resultant dish, made from the fattened liver, *iecur ficatum* or "fig liver." These days French geese and ducks are force-fed corn rather than figs, but, interestingly, the French word for liver, *foie*, derives from *ficatum* ("fig"), so closely was animal liver formerly associated with this practice. The French—who are now the main producers in the world (although Hungary comes a close second), with an estimated annual output of around twenty-five thousand tons of foie gras—claim the birds grow to enjoy their extra daily ration of corn being pushed down their throats through a funnel. A rather different insight is offered by Charles Gérard, in his *Ancienne Alsace à table*, published in 1877 (at this point animal lovers should look away): "The goose is nothing, but man has made of it an instrument for the output of a marvelous product, a kind of living hothouse within which there grows the supreme fruit of gastronomy." It's OK, you can all look back now.

6
Salads and Vegetables

What Did Caesar Do for My Salad?

A Favorite Salad from the Waldorf Hotel

Coleslaw: Do You Prefer Your Salad Cold
or with Cabbage?

Robert H. Cobb: Salad Maker to the Stars

What Are the Right Ingredients for a Nice Salad?

Sauerkraut and the Seaman's Disease

Brussels Sprouts: The Vegetable We All Love to Hate

Pease Pudding Hot: What Did Ordinary Folk
Eat in the Middle Ages?

Did the French Invent Baked Beans?

The Rise and Fall of the Potato

The Original Celebrity Chef—Ramsey,
Eat Your Celery Heart Out!

A Vegetarian Delight, Thanks to World War II

Colcannon: How a Spoonful of
Mash Could Win You a Husband

There was an Old Person of Fife,
Who was greatly disgusted with life;
They sang him a ballad,
And fed him on salad,
Which cured that Old Person of Fife.

EDWARD LEAR

What I say is that, if a fellow really likes potatoes, he
must be a pretty decent sort of fellow.

A. A. MILNE

What Did Caesar Do for My Salad?

The name, of course, conjures up a grumpy, toga-clad emperor tucking into a bit of lunch before perhaps throwing a Christian or two to the lions, in the name of entertainment, to keep the people of Rome happy. But instead it turns out that **Caesar salad** is less than a hundred years old and comes from the most unlikely of places, Mexico.

Caesar Cardini (1896–1956) was born in Italy and emigrated to America with his three brothers at the beginning of World War I. It was the era of Prohibition—also known as the Noble Experiment—when between 1920 and 1933 the sale, manufacture, and transportation of alcohol was banned in the United States. The aim was to improve morality and behavior, but in fact it just encouraged a huge rise in organized crime. Realizing what lengths people would go to, just to have a drink or two, Caesar and his brother Alex saw a legal business opportunity and seized hold of it. In 1924, they moved a short distance across the Mexican border, from Los Angeles, and set up a restaurant in Tijuana after the town became a firm favorite for southern Californians looking for a weekend party.

The Cardinis' combination of strong alcohol and tasty Italian food proved to be a winner, and their Fourth of July celebrations were so oversubscribed that, according to Caesar's daughter Rosa, her father soon ran out of ingredients to feed his drunken customers. He responded by throwing together a salad of basically whatever he had left in the kitchen: lettuce, croutons, PARMESAN CHEESE, eggs, olive oil, lemon juice, BLACK PEPPER, and WORCESTERSHIRE SAUCE. Perhaps trying to make up for his dish's simplicity, he brought the salad to the table, and with a theatrical flourish, tossed it in front of his customers so that every leaf was covered in the thick dressing.

The story goes that the dish proved so popular with a group of partying Hollywood film stars who had flown in for the weekend that Alex named it "Aviator salad," in their honor. Later, once their restaurant was established on the ground floor of the Hotel Commercial, the Cardinis could afford to admit the truth and the salad was renamed after Caesar and soon became a favorite among the stars of the day, who demanded the dish wherever they traveled in the world.

But while Caesar salad isn't centuries old, it turns out that the Romans were equally enthusiastic about eating raw leaves. Much like their modern counterparts, these salads would have consisted of a selection of leaves, including arugula, watercress, mallow, sorrel, goosefoot, purslane, chicory, beet greens, celery, chervil, basil, and other fresh herbs. Our very word derives from the Latin name *salata herba*, literally "salted herbs," which shows that both Julius Caesar and Caesar Cardini had a similar taste in strongly flavored dressings. Thanks to his impromptu way of dressing a salad, Caesar Cardini became a rich man and eventually trademarked his famous creation, in 1948. Today the Cardini company remains a producer of an ever-growing range of oils and dressings.

A Favorite Salad from the Waldorf Hotel

Waldorf salad—chopped apple and celery mixed with grapes and walnuts in a smooth MAYONNAISE dressing—was created in 1893 at the Waldorf Hotel in New York (now the Waldorf-Astoria Hotel). According to one theory, the iconic salad was originally devised by the Waldorf Lunch System, an early twentieth-century lunchroom chain whose company logo was an apple. But it goes back further than this, the recipe first appearing in 1896 in *The Cook Book by "Oscar" of the Waldorf*. In what must be one of the earliest Christmas cookbook-type fads, the hotel's maître d,' Oscar Tschirky (see also EGGS BENEDICT and THOUSAND ISLAND DRESSING), is credited with persuading his head chef to include his favorite salad on the hotel menu.

Over the years it has become one of America's most popular dishes. In Cole Porter's "You're the Top," from the musical *Anything Goes*, the singer compares his beloved to all the best things in the world: the smile of the Mona Lisa, the steps of Fred Astaire, Mickey Mouse, Mahatma Gandhi . . . and a Waldorf salad.

Coleslaw: Do You Prefer Your Salad Cold or with Cabbage?

Consisting chiefly of shredded cabbage and carrot dressed with MAYONNAISE, **coleslaw** originated in America in the late seventeenth and early eighteenth centuries, when Dutch immigrants flooded into the country. Indeed, New York was originally called New Amsterdam because of the sheer number of Dutch settlers who ended up there. The colonists brought with them their favorite recipe for salad, *koolsla* (from *kool*, "cabbage," and *sla*, "salad"), which over the following two centuries became anglicized to "coleslaw." But there was initially some confusion as to whether it should indeed be "coleslaw" or "cold slaw." As English became the common language in America, people lost sight of the original derivation of *kool*, believing the word meant "cool" and hence it must be a "cold" rather than a "cabbage" salad. A record from 1794 bears this out, describing "a piece of sliced cabbage, by Dutchman ycleped [called] cold slaw." In England, however, where the dish had become popular in the early nineteenth century, the correct form of the term was adopted quite quickly as "cole"—denoting plants of the *Brassica* genus—which was already associated with cabbage.

Robert H. Cobb: Salad Maker to the Stars

Robert H. Cobb—cousin of the baseball legend Ty Cobb, the first player to enter the Hall of Fame in 1936—was a co-founder of the celebrated Brown Derby chain of restaurants in Los Angeles, California, established in 1926 and synonymous with the Golden Age of Hollywood. The first Brown Derby restaurant, built on Wilshire Boulevard, is actually shaped like a derby hat (a bowler hat, in other words), a design thought to have been inspired by Cobb's business partner, Gloria Swanson's husband Herbert Somborn, in response to being told that a good restaurateur could "serve food out of a hat and still make a success of it." The restaurant was an instant success, its quirky shape attracting diners from all over Los Angeles, and soon there was a small chain of Brown Derbys across the city.

What Robert Cobb is chiefly remembered for, however, is his great **Cobb salad**. Late one night, back in 1937—so the story goes—he was visited by his friend the showman Sidney

Grauman, owner of the legendary Grauman's Chinese Theatre on Hollywood Boulevard. Grauman was feeling peckish, and as the chefs had already left, Cobb offered to rustle something up for him. Rummaging through the fridge, he grabbed some lettuce, tomatoes, avocado, BACON, chicken, and Roquefort cheese, chopped them all finely, added a hard-boiled egg, and served the resulting dish to his friend. Grauman was so delighted with his midnight snack that he always ordered it when dining in a Brown Derby, and word soon spread throughout Hollywood.

Cobb's wife, however, told a different story: about how her husband had returned hungry from a long and painful trip to the dentist and asked his head chef for something he would be able to eat. The chef chose ingredients he knew his boss enjoyed, chopping them up finely so that he could eat them easily with a swollen mouth, and Cobb loved the resulting salad so much he added it to the menu in all his restaurants. Whichever version of events is right, there's no doubting that the dish can now be found on restaurant menus the world over.

What Are the Right Ingredients for a Nice Salad?

As the name suggests, **salade Niçoise** is, quite simply, a salad from Nice, in southern France, and it is made up of locally sourced ingredients—anchovies, garlic, tomatoes, black olives, and capers in a vinaigrette dressing. As Nice is a coastal city—and the second most visited in France after Paris—fish feature prominently in its cuisine. Like Marseilles, it is known for its own version of the fish stew BOUILLABAISSE, while anchovies, in particular, appear in several dishes, including the savory tart *pissaladière* (the word derives

from *pissalat*, "salted fish"—in case you're wondering). Indeed,
fish are used to such an extent locally that it has given rise to
a saying: "Fish are born in the sea and die in oil" (olive oil
being ubiquitous in Mediterranean cooking). Rumor has it
that the dish was developed by the celebrated Russian chore-
ographer George Balanchine (1904–83) while he was based
in Monte Carlo, just along the coast from Nice. However,
although Balanchine was a great arranger of dancers, it's not
known whether he had the same gift with vegetables or indeed
fish. The salad is in fact a traditional southern French dish,
the only matter for dispute being about exactly which ingredients should be included, potatoes, tuna, and green beans
being regarded by purists as unwelcome interlopers.

Sauerkraut and the Seaman's Disease

The archetypal German dish, **sauerkraut** means "pickled
cabbage" (literally "sour cabbage") and that's exactly what it
is. Luckily its history turns out to be rather more complex.
As pickling food goes back to at least the third century BC—
the ancient Greeks were extremely partial to pickled olives—it
has been commonly supposed that sauerkraut is just as ancient.
But while, in ancient times, pickles were "wet"—made by adding ingredients to salted water (brine)—sauerkraut is dry-salted,

the salt drawing all the liquid out of the cabbage, which is then preserved and flavored by fermentation. Although the Romans were very fond of cabbage, crediting it with many health-giving properties, they used the latter process only to make long-lasting cattlefeed rather than anything for their own consumption.

Sauerkraut was first produced in Germany around the sixteenth century, and first mentioned in print a century later. Whoever the absent-minded farmer was who first tried eating it this way, the key upside was that, unlike wet-pickling, this method preserved much of the vitamin C in the cabbage. For a seventeenth-century peasant whose limited diet became even more so in the winter, sauerkraut would have made a vital difference to whether he actually survived until spring. It wasn't until three centuries later, in 1932, that vitamin C was identified as an essential nutrient; what was recognized, however, were the effects of its absence.

First noted by Hippocrates in the fourth century BC, scurvy—caused by insufficient vitamin C in the diet—often killed large numbers of the passengers and crew on long-distance voyages, in which fresh vegetables were generally in short supply. This became a significant issue in Europe from the fifteenth century, the beginning of the Age of Discovery. Magellan, for example, lost 80 percent of his crew to the disease when crossing the Pacific.

Scurvy first came to public notice in Britain in the 1740s when Commodore George Anson led a squadron on a disastrous mission to the Pacific. He lost all but one of his six ships, and two-thirds of the entire crew (700 survived out of his original complement of 2,000), most to scurvy. Their symptoms were vividly described by the expedition chaplain, Richard Walter, who wrote the official account of the voyage, describing blackened skin, ulcers, difficulty breathing, rictus of the limbs, teeth falling out, and an overgrowth of gum tissue that rotted, lending the victim's breath a foul odor. But perhaps worst of all were the delusions and madness sufferers underwent. Walter describes Anson's ships as echoing with the weeping and screaming of those stricken with the disease.

The British navy in its determination to rule the waves became obsessed with trying to stamp out scurvy. The most famous advocate of sauerkraut as a preventative for it was Captain James Cook (1728–79), who took enormous pains to persuade his men to eat what he called "sour crout." He would eat it alongside them, deliberately enthusing about how good it was. Cook recognized, as he noted in his journals, the sailors' instinctive distaste for anything "out of the Common way, although it be ever so much for their own good" and how, by contrast, what "their Superiors set a Value on . . . becomes the finest stuff in the World."

As a result, only five cases of scurvy were reported by the ship's surgeon during Cook's first voyage and no deaths from it. In his next two voyages, Cook's good management, or luck, persisted, and still no deaths from scurvy were reported. He was consequently hailed by the British as the conqueror of the sea's great plague, his victory reflected by William Bowles in his poem *The Spirit of Discovery* (1804):

> Smile, glowing health! For now no more the wasted
>   seaman sinks,
> With haggard eye and feeble frame diseased;
> No more with tortured longings for the sight
> Of fields and hillocks green, madly he calls.

Lemons have been known since ancient times as a far better preventative of scurvy, but in the eighteenth century they had to be imported and the supplies were extremely unreliable and expensive—unlike the much less romantic cabbage. During the nineteenth century, and in order to combat the disease, a concentrated drink made from lime juice was introduced by the Royal Navy as part of a seaman's daily ration. British sailors became so associated with it that it gave rise to the nickname *Limeys*, still in use today and applied, typically by Americans, to Brits of all kinds, not just seamen. German mariners, by contrast, continued to eat their national dish, earning themselves the nickname *Krauts*. In the early twentieth century, meanwhile, following the outbreak of World War I, sauerkraut was briefly rechristened **liberty cabbage** by American manufacturers in a spate of renaming that extended to a number of other foods (see also FRENCH TOAST and SALISBURY STEAK).

Brussels Sprouts: The Vegetable We All Love to Hate

Supporters of the almost universally disliked **Brussels sprout** claim that, cooked correctly, they are delicious and that the dislike stems from overcooking, as it releases the glucosinolate singrin, which gives out the sulphurous odor redolent of canteens in Hell. Detractors, on the other hand, maintain there is no correct way to cook them. Jane Grigson in her *Vegetable Book* (1978) suggests that sprouts have been grown in Belgium since the Middle Ages, even featuring at wedding feasts of the Burgundian court in the fifteenth century, but that mysteriously they didn't catch on, not becoming known outside Belgian borders until the end of the eighteenth century. Luckily for Belgian national pride, the country has managed to redeem its culinary reputation with its simultaneous invention and perfection of FRENCH FRIES.

Pease Pudding Hot: What Did Ordinary Folk Eat in the Middle Ages?

It is the humble pea that, for hundreds of years, provided the foundation of the traditional English peasant's diet. Derived from the Latin *pisum*, the word was originally anglicized as "pease," eventually evolving into "pea" in the singular. **Pease pudding**, made with yellow split peas and similar in color and texture to HUMMUS, was part of the everyday diet for generations of country folk. Peas were easy to grow and made ideal food, along with lentils and beans, for one-pot peasant cooking, especially as they could be dried and preserved for long periods.

A pot of yellowish sludge might sound unappetizing, but the lower classes of medieval England actually had a healthier diet than their noble counterparts. Peasant food was largely homegrown: fresh herbs and vegetables from their own plots, nuts and fruit from local trees, some meat (so long as it wasn't hunted—any poaching could result in death or having their hands cut off), wholegrain bread, and dairy products. The upper classes, by contrast, disdained most vegetables, as they came from the ground and were therefore only fit to feed the poor, and ate only white bread, as they considered it more refined (which it was, if only in a literal sense). They ate meat and fish aplenty and, after the Crusades opened up trade further east, liked everything heavily spiced. Needless to say, this led to a whole range of health problems, including skin diseases, rickets, and scurvy (see SAUERKRAUT).

In the light of this, the nutrient-laden pea begins to sound a little more glamorous. After being introduced to Britain— probably by the Vikings, as it is a traditional Swedish vegetable—peas would regularly be cooked, usually with salted (preserved) BACON, in the form of pease pudding (also known as **pease porridge**). And it is still made today: although now rarely mentioned in the south of England, it remains popular in the north, where it can be purchased in canned form. Two centuries ago, pease pudding was still such a part of the English way of life that children would sing about it in a nursery rhyme, originally published in 1760 in John Newberry's *Mother Goose's Melody*:

> Pease porridge hot, pease porridge cold,
> Pease porridge in the pot, nine days old;
> Some like it hot, some like it cold,
> Some like it in the pot, nine days old.

Did the French Invent Baked Beans?

Anyone who's seen the classic scene in Mel Brooks's comic western *Blazing Saddles*, where the cowboys sit around the campfire eating **baked beans** and farting copiously, will be convinced it is an American dish through and through. Supporting this is the theory of some food historians that baked beans are based on a Native American dish consisting of beans cooked with bear fat and maple syrup. The French, on the other hand, maintain that the dish can be traced to their classic bean stew, **cassoulet**, which they say they introduced to the Americans while fighting alongside them during the Revolutionary War of 1775–83 (see FRENCH FRIES and TEA). But, given that the haricot beans integral to the American recipe are native to the United States and that most cultures have independently developed their own recipe for bean stews, that seems a pretty tenuous claim to me.

What is certain is that America has made the baked bean its own. The name of the dish is a reminder of how it was traditionally cooked—baked in a ceramic or cast-iron pot.

The expression **full of beans** is regularly applied to anyone behaving in a lively and energetic manner. A similar expression, **feeling his oats**—evoking the friskiness of a recently fed horse—provides a clue to the origin of the first phrase. The Romans are recorded to have used beans as fodder for their horses—known accordingly as "horse beans." Hence any well-fed and energetic horse was regarded as "full of beans."

Bean-hole cooking, as practiced in logging camps in the northeast, used a stone-lined fire pit in which the bean pot would be buried overnight to cook. Historically, America's baked bean "capital" was Boston, where beans slow-baked in molasses were so popular the city was nicknamed "Beantown."

With the invention of the can, beans were among the first convenience foods. During the Civil War in the 1860s, the army was fed on canned salted pork and beans with stewed tomatoes. Henry Heinz launched his baked beans in 1895 and brought them to the UK nine years later.

The Rise and Fall of the Potato

As with the tomato (see GAZPACHO), it's hard to imagine a time when the **potato** wasn't a fundamental ingredient in cooking, but this root vegetable—the most versatile of all—wasn't introduced into Europe until the sixteenth century. At first many Europeans were suspicious of the potato, believing it to contain harmful poisons. To be fair, there was some justification, as it is from the same family as deadly nightshade, which is poisonous raw. In 1748, the French Parliament actually banned cultivation of the crop, believing it to cause leprosy, among other things, while during the 1770s, a period of recurrent famines, wagonloads of potatoes sent by Frederick the Great of Prussia were rejected by starving peasants, but attitudes soon began to change, thanks to the efforts of one man.

PARMENTIER: CHAMPION OF THE POTATO

Antoine-Augustin Parmentier (1737–1813) was an army chemist who was captured no less than five times by Prussian forces during the Seven Years' War (1756–63). In captivity, Parmentier and his fellow prisoners of war were forced to survive on a diet of potatoes and so, with plenty of time on his hands, the scientist began a detailed study of this unpopular food. When the Academy of Besançon later sponsored a competition to find a "food capable of reducing the calamities of famine," Parmentier submitted his paper, "The Chemical Explanation of the Potato," and won first prize.

Parmentier then spent the rest of his life promoting the humble spud throughout Europe as a cheap, nutritious, and reliable crop, and in 1785 finally managed to persuade Louis XVI (1754–93) to encourage cultivation in France. The king allowed him to plant one hundred acres on royal land, close to Paris, and Parmentier engaged a heavily armed guard to protect the crop. This strange move aroused the curiosity of local farmers, who became desperate to know more about this obviously valuable crop, and as word spread among the puzzled population, Parmentier delivered what turned out to be his masterstroke. He dismissed the armed guard and, as he anticipated, the French flocked into the fields, dug up the potatoes, and replanted them in their own farms and gardens.

The habit of growing potatoes then quickly spread throughout the continent, such that by the time of the onset of the French Revolution in 1789, they were a staple in the diet of every French family, including that of the soon-to-be-headless king and his queen, Marie Antoinette, who were both known for their love of potatoes. (So much so in the case of Marie Antoinette that she even wore a headdress of potato flowers at a fancy-dress ball.) And for this, the name of Antoine-Augustin Parmentier has become synonymous with the potato in France. Indeed, many potato-based recipes are named after him—including **hachis Parmentier**, a form of French COTTAGE or SHEPHERD'S PIE.

HOW THE POTATO KILLED A MILLION PEOPLE

But one European country had already been turned on to the benefit of the potato: Ireland. Sir Walter Raleigh (1552–1618), the British explorer known for his expeditions to the Americas and for throwing his best cloak across a puddle so Elizabeth I could walk across it, had introduced potatoes to Ireland, planting them at his Irish estate at Myrtle Grove, Youghal, near Cork. Legend has it that he then invited the local gentry to a banquet featuring potatoes in every course. Unfortunately, his cooks, who knew nothing about the vegetable, tossed out the tubers, bringing to the table a poisonous dish of boiled stems and leaves instead, which promptly made his noble guests extremely ill.

Unlike in France, where the potato worked its way from the top of society down, in Ireland its popularity grew from the bottom up. Ireland's rain-soaked climate meant that few crops prospered, and before the seventeenth century, its peasants depended very heavily on oats. Offering two-to-four times the calories of grain per acre, and much simpler to cook, potatoes rapidly took over as the country's main crop. The Irish became known for their expertise in cooking them: the favorite street snack of eighteenth-century London was the **baked potato**, preferably cooked and sold by an Irishman, although its popularity was eclipsed in the nineteenth century by another Irish potato speciality, the chip (see FISH AND CHIPS and FRENCH FRIES).

The problem was that the Irish put all their eggs (or rather potatoes) in one basket. Depending so heavily on a single crop meant that one bad harvest represented a catastrophe. And when one bad harvest turned into four, people started dying in the thousands. At the height of the famine (around 1845), at least 1 million people died of starvation, leaving many poverty-stricken families with no choice but to emigrate. Towns became deserted and many businesses closed: with no customers, shop owners were forced to leave, too. Over 1.5 million people sailed for North America and Australia, and within a few years Ireland's population had dropped by half, from around 9 million to little more than 4 million. And it was all because of the potato.

The Original Celebrity Chef—Ramsey, Eat Your Celery Heart Out!

This classic of celery hearts is simmered in chicken stock and served with peppers on a bed of crisp lettuce. Victor Hertzler (1875–1935) is considered to be the first of the high-profile American chefs who successfully publicized himself and his kitchen at the St. Francis Hotel in San Francisco by writing cookbooks; hosting vast, elaborate meals; and inventing dishes that he named after prominent hotel guests and friends. Hertzler was born in France and learned his craft at the Grand Hotel in Paris before moving to the Waldorf Hotel in New York, which, at the time, was the largest hotel in the world. In 1904, he was invited to become chef at the new St. Francis Hotel in San Francisco and made his name in 1906 when the hotel was one of the few buildings to survive the devastating earthquake that virtually destroyed the city and left around half of the residents homeless.

The St. Francis Hotel became a sanctuary for many, as Hertzler opened for breakfast as usual within an hour of what was to be America's worst natural disaster until Hurricane Katrina leveled New Orleans in 2005. As San Francisco burned, Hertzler remained calm and served an Earthquake Survivor Breakfast, a tradition that would be repeated every year at the hotel in honor of the victims. In 2006, the hotel marked the one hundredth anniversary of the earthquake by, once again, reproducing Hertzler's original breakfast menu, and diners toasted to the memory of the little Frenchman who, with his trademark mustache, pointed beard, and red fez hat, had become so familiar in San Francisco a century earlier.

In addition to inventing **celery Victor**, the chef is also credited with **eggs Moscow**, an egg dish stuffed with caviar, and **eggs Sarah Bernhardt** after the legendary French stage actress, otherwise known as "the Divine Sarah." Bernhardt had stayed at the St. Francis Hotel during her successful tour of the United States in 1915. Victor Hertzler is also thought to be responsible for another famous dish, **crab Louie salad**, otherwise known as "the king of salads," and the Caruso cocktail after the legendary Italian tenor Enrico Caruso, who sought sanctuary at the hotel after the great earthquake had damaged his suite at the nearby Palace Hotel before fleeing San Francisco, never to return.

The St. Francis Hotel was the scene of Hollywood's first great scandal when, in 1921, Fatty Arbuckle hosted a party in his suite, a raucous affair that led to the death of a young actress named Virginia Rappe. Newspaper headlines all over the country reported "Girl Dead in Wild Party at Hotel," and other guests pointed the finger firmly at Arbuckle himself, who stood trial for murder in December. Arbuckle was acquitted by a jury that was unable to reach a verdict, and although he survived a retrial when a second jury was also unable to agree, his career lay in tatters. The most popular American actor of his generation never worked again, and his films were withdrawn, an event remembered as the first example of the censorship of American motion pictures.

A Vegetarian Delight, Thanks to World War II

As Britain braced itself for food shortages during World War II, the British government asked a number of London chefs to produce a list of recipes containing cheap, easily available, and nutritious foods to be recommended to the public. Francis Latry, chef at the Savoy Hotel in London, responded with a pie of cauliflower, rutabaga, carrots, parsnip, and onion with either a pastry or potato crust, grated cheese, and brown gravy. A vegetarian delight! The British people, however, needed persuading, and it fell to the Minister for Food, Frederick Marquis, 1st Lord Woolton (1883–1964), to do the convincing, as the *Times* duly noted:

> When Woolton Pie was being forced upon reluctant tables, Lord Woolton performed a valuable service by allowing photographs to be taken whilst eating, at public

luncheons, with every sign of enjoyment, the dish named after him.

These were the days when public figures could indeed influence the general public—we can only imagine the reaction one might expect these days if he were to try to convince youngsters to eat a basic vegetable pie. But those were different times indeed, and **Woolton pie** became a staple of the British diet during the period of food rationing between 1940 and 1954, especially as housewives could, quite literally, grow it in the garden.

Prior to the war, Lord Woolton was the managing director of a department store and was awarded his peerage in 1938 for his services to British industry. He served on a number of government committees but refused to associate himself with any particular political party and remained fiercely independent. In 1940, he was appointed Minister for Food by Prime Minister Neville Chamberlain, a position he retained when Winston Churchill took over. Responsible for food rationing, Woolton was pragmatic and succeeded in difficult circumstances by taking the view that the people must be kept fully informed by a strong advertising campaign highlighting the obvious food shortages, a move that ensured his own personal popularity and a famous vegetable pie named in his honor.

Colcannon: How a Spoonful of Mash Could Win You a Husband

Colcannon is a traditional Irish dish made of mashed potatoes mixed with cabbage. Simple fare, in other words, sometimes flavored with cream, butter, garlic, or BACON, although such luxuries were rarely available during harsher times. The name of the dish comes from the Gaelic *cál ceannann*, meaning "white cabbage," although there is evidence to suggest that "cannon" evolved from the Older Irish *cainnenn*, translated variously as onion, garlic, or leek.

Other countries have similar versions of the dish. In England, for instance, leftover potatoes and vegetables (often from the SUNDAY ROAST), plus a bit of cold meat, are chopped up and shallow-fried as **bubble and squeak**—the name deriving from the sound the ingredients make when being heated. In Scotland, shredded onion and cabbage are mixed with mashed potatoes and baked with a topping of cheese into the splendidly named **rumbledethumps**, suggesting particularly vigorous cooking—or a rather bad-tempered chef.

In Ireland, a ring or a small coin would traditionally be hidden in a dish of colcannon and the lucky girl who found it in her helping would be the next to receive a marriage proposal. Following another custom, unmarried girls would hang a sock filled with spoonfuls of colcannon above the front door on the night of Halloween, in the belief that the next man to pass through the door would be their future husband—making that a popular evening for village idiots across the land. But a word of warning: if somebody invites you to their house at Halloween and you see a bulging sock outside the front door, make sure you know what their daughter looks like before you ring the bell.

7
The Fish Course

"Oh, as to the whiting," said the Mock Turtle, "they—you've seen them, of course?"

"Yes," said Alice, "I've often seen them at dinn–" she checked herself hastily.

"I don't know where Dinn may be," said the Mock Turtle; "but, if you've seen them so often, of course you know what they're like?"

"I believe so," Alice replied thoughtfully. "They have their tails in their mouths—and they're all over crumbs."

LEWIS CARROLL, *Alice's Adventures in Wonderland*

Lobster Thermidor: A Luxury Dish with a Revolutionary History

Consisting of lobster meat mixed with egg yolks and brandy, served in a lobster shell, often with cheese on top, **lobster Thermidor** is an extremely expensive dish, eaten mostly by the wealthy and privileged. So you may be surprised to learn that its name derives from a period in French history when wealth and privilege were very much under attack.

The French Revolution (1789–99) arose out of a strong feeling of discontent among the working people, fueled by widespread famine and the near bankruptcy of the nation following a series of ruinous wars. As the revolutionaries saw it, the ruling classes of France had had all the power and all the money for far too long; they were determined to establish a new world order that would change everything, even down to the way things were measured. A simpler, standardized method would be adopted, in which everything would be in multiples of ten. And so the metric system came into being, first taken up by France and now, of course, employed internationally. Rather less successful was the attempt to apply the same system to the way in which time was recorded. Each day was divided into ten hours each consisting of one hundred minutes. Each month now lasted three weeks and the weeks were each ten days long, while their old, elitist names (July and August were named after Roman emperors, Julian and Augustus) were replaced by utilitarian words referring to the weather or nature, such as Pluviôse, Ventôse, and Floréal ("Rainy," "Foggy," and "Flowery"). Thermidor, from the Greek *thermos* or "hot," was, as the name suggests, a summer month, lasting from July 20 to August 18 in the old terminology.

The problem arose when these ideas didn't end up working in practice, the ideals of the newly established Republic—liberty, equality, and fraternity—little more than empty rhetoric. After the execution of the French king, in 1793, there were food riots and civil unrest and the Republicans imposed what came to be known as the Reign of Terror. Maximilien Robespierre (1758–94) was the guiding force behind it, believing the Terror to be wholly necessary as a means of keeping France on the straight and narrow by rooting out so-called traitors. Revolutionary France rapidly turned into a paranoid dictatorship: anyone who stepped out of line or disagreed with the increasingly unstable leadership was summarily executed. On Thermidor 9, Year II (July 27, 1794), disaffected members of the National Convention, the Republican government, arrested Robespierre and executed him without trial. "Thermidor" has come to indicate the "cooling off" phase in any revolution, when power slips from the hands of the original revolutionary leadership and radicals are replaced by a more conservative regime, sometimes to the point where the political pendulum may swing back to its prerevolutionary position.

So how did it come to be applied to a dish? According to one theory, lobster Thermidor was created by a French chef in honor of Napoleon Bonaparte (1769–1821)—the perfect example, you might say, of how far the political pendulum may swing back, for Napoleon not only ruled France like a king but crowned himself emperor in 1804. It is said that his chef suggested "lobster Napoleon" but the diminutive Frenchman insisted the dish should be associated instead with the coup de Thermidor. As the recipe didn't appear in print until the 1890s, however, it seems unlikely a full hundred years would have passed before anybody recorded it. It is also unlikely that a man as vain and egotistical as Napoleon would decline the honor of having a dish named after him, and even less likely that he would name it after a point in recent history marking the downfall of a power-crazed dictator.

A more plausible story suggests that the dish was created at the Café de Paris to mark the opening night of a new play by Victorien Sardou (1831–1908) at the Comédie Française theater in January 1891. A few years earlier, in 1887, Sardou's play *La Tosca*, on which the celebrated opera by Puccini is based, had made him famous. In honor of Sardou, the chef at the Café de Paris, Tony Girod, created a lobster dish that he named after the new play. *Thermidor* dramatized Robespierre's downfall and the difficulties of maintaining revolutionary ideals in the face of reality: unfortunately, like the Republican month it was named after, it was not a success, and if it weren't for Tony Girod's (rather more digestible) cheesy lobster dish, it would be completely forgotten today.

The Magnificent Delmonico's and the Cuban Connection

Ben Wenberg was a wealthy ship owner and merchant who worked the Cuba to New York fruit trade routes during the mid-1800s. He and his younger brother, Louis, became prominent and well-liked New York society gents and were frequent visitors to Delmonico's Restaurant on William Street, owned by Lorenz Delmonico and run by his nephew Charles. The restaurant had already established itself as one of America's finest by the time chef Charles Ranhofer took over the running of the kitchens in 1862, but the Frenchman made the place world famous with a series of signature dishes. In 1876, Ben Wenberg returned from one of his voyages with a new recipe for lobster, considered to be food for the poor in those days.

Wenberg demonstrated the dish to Delmonico and Ranhofer, who were immediately taken by the unique taste, thanks to spices such as cayenne pepper, and the restaurant soon added Wenberg's creation as lobster à la Wenberg to the menu, instantly proving popular with the city's after-theater diners. Shortly afterward, however, Wenberg and Delmonico argued over a trivial matter and the merchant was banned from the restaurant altogether. Delmonico also ordered the lobster dish to be removed from the menu, causing an outcry among diners who repeatedly demanded the meal. Ranhofer was forced to reintroduce the dish as lobster à la Delmonico, but it failed to attract diners in the same way as its predecessor, so Delmonico reluctantly agreed to put it back on his menu after reversing the first and third letters and calling it **lobster Newberg**. Close enough, he felt, to appease customers but without honoring his former friend. By the time Wenberg died of pneumonia, coincidently during the same week as his brother in June 1885, his recipe had become one of the most famous lobster dishes in the country. Lobster Newberg first appeared in Ranhofer's recipe book *The Epicurean*, published in 1894.

Ranhofer had a flair for creating new dishes, and Delmonico's enjoyed honoring their favorite customers and national events. Between them they are responsible for **baked Alaska**, to commemorate the purchase of Alaska from the Russian Empire in 1867; **veal pie à la Dickens**, after the famous author's favorite food; **Sarah potatoes**, in honor of legendary actress and customer Sarah Bernhardt; **salad à la Dumas**, after Ranhofer's favorite author, Alexandre Dumas, creator of *The Three Musketeers* (1843) and *The Count of Monte Cristo* (1844); and a popular dessert called **peach pudding à la Cleveland**, for two-time president Grover Cleveland (1885–1899 and 1893–1897).

The Recipe with the Richest Secret in America

Though it's one of the most famous oyster recipes in the world, the actual ingredients of **oysters Rockefeller** are said to be a closely guarded secret. The dish was created in America's oldest family-run restaurant, Antoine's in New Orleans, established by Antoine Alciatore in 1840. Oysters Rockefeller was created by Antoine's son, Jules Alciatore, in 1899 using what is thought to be a puree of spinach, parsley, butter, and breadcrumbs and has been replicated by restaurants across the world, although Antoine's claims never to have revealed the actual recipe and that no other restaurant has successfully repeated their signature dish.

The original recipe has been handed down from father to son for five generations, never having left the family, although a laboratory analysis in 1986 revealed parsley, celery, and chives were the principal ingredients. Antoine's, by then run by fifth-generation family owner Roy Guste, made no comment on the laboratory findings. What is known is that the dish is rich and green, said to resemble a dollar bill. To emphasize how rich the sauce was, Jules Alciatore named the dish—created simply because a shortage of snails in the summer of 1899 forced the chef to substitute them with oysters on the specials menu—after the richest man in the world at the time, John D. Rockefeller.

Rockefeller was born in 1837, the second of six children of William Avery Rockefeller, a traveling salesman, and his wife, Eliza Davidson. The young Rockefeller dreamed of becoming a musician, though he showed a natural aptitude for math and at the age of sixteen joined a small firm of accountants called Hewitt and Tuttle as an assistant bookkeeper. At the end of his first month's work, in what should be an example to all of us, Rockefeller donated 6 percent of his salary to charity, a habit he continued every single month of his life, increasing it to 10 percent by the time he was twenty years old.

In 1859, Rockefeller went into partnership with Maurice B. Clarke commissioning produce and soon noticed whale oil, used for lighting and heating, was becoming too expensive. As the Civil War broke out in 1861, the demand for oil increased, and in 1863, Rockefeller was in a position to build an oil refinery, one of only five in the United States, that would later become the Rockefeller-owned Standard Oil Company. Rockefeller earned millions supplying oil to the growing shipping industry and to industry around the world, and by 1899, the year his famous oyster dish was created, Rockefeller was thought to be the richest man in the world. Henry T. Ford's gas-run motorcar then created the modern petroleum industry, and by the time Rockefeller died just two months short of his ninety-eighth birthday, the oil magnate had been the richest man on the planet for over forty years, giving away over $600 million to good causes in the process.

Oysters Rockefeller will probably live on forever, unless the good folks at Antoine's make their famous sauce even richer and start calling it oysters Gates. Antoine's Restaurant is also responsible for **eggs Sardou**, a dish of poached eggs with creamed spinach, artichoke, and hollandaise sauce created for the prolific French playwright Victorien Sardou, who was responsible for seventy-one stage plays and two books during his fifty-year career that began in 1855. Sardou's best-known work is *La Tosca*, although he was also responsible for *Thermidor* (see LOBSTER THERMIDOR), and *Fedora*, a play that would later have a famous hat named after it.

The Legendary Days of a
Golden Hollywood Era

The famous Café La Maze was created in 1935 when Marcel Lamaze opened the doors to his new establishment on Sunset Boulevard in Los Angeles. Lamaze advertised his new café as the "Hangout of the Stars," and surprisingly, some of the movie legends of the Golden Era of Hollywood did become regular customers. Lamaze was soon playing poker with the Marx Brothers and rubbing elbows with the likes of Jimmy Durante and Errol Flynn. Prohibition, a law that banned the sale of alcohol between 1920 and 1933, had led to the small town of Tijuana in northern Mexico (see CAESAR SALAD) becoming a resort for the rich and famous as southern Californians flooded out of America to eat, drink, and generally have a good time. Hollywood stars became a regular feature, as did restaurateurs, and Marcel Lamaze was soon encouraged to open a second café in San Diego, a few minutes up the road from the Mexican playground.

Marcel Lamaze was born in Providence, Rhode Island, despite claiming to have been born in France for reasons I cannot imagine, and began his career in the restaurant industry at George Rector's Restaurant in New York (see SOLE MARGUERY) before moving to make his name on the West Coast. After achieving success with his restaurants, and the recognition of the Hollywood jet set, Lamaze opened the doors to his new Café La Maze in National City in 1940 to a blaze of publicity, thanks to the owner's new friends Bing Crosby, Clarke Gable, and Johnny Weissmuller all being photographed there. Let's face it, having Tarzan at the opening of your restaurant is bound to cause a stir. Over the following years the Hollywood elite would drive out to National

City, enjoy an evening illegally gambling in Lamaze's secret upstairs gaming room, and then head out for Tijuana the following morning.

Although **shrimp Lamaze** had become a signature dish at both the Los Angeles and San Diego cafés, there is a twist to this otherwise simple story. George Lamaze, Marcel's brother, was also a well-known and well-connected restaurant and hotel owner responsible for a number of high-profile and fashionable locations, including the prestigious Warwick Hotel in Philadelphia, which he took over in 1935. Relatives of Lamaze's chef at the time, Johann Lamprecht, claim the hotel chef invented shrimp Lamaze himself, in honor of his friend and employer. While this is probably true, there were small differences in the recipes between Marcel's and George's menus, suggesting Marcel modified it before including it on his own menu. Either way, shrimp Lamaze remains on menus as a constant reminder of the legendary hotel and restaurant owners of the Golden State.

The expression **red herring** is used to describe something that provides a false or misleading clue, often in a detective story. In the eighteenth and nineteenth centuries, herring was one of the most widely caught fish in the seas around Britain. In the days before refrigeration, it would have been preserved by salting and smoking to ensure it was still edible by the time it arrived at market towns inland. The smoking process would turn the herring a deep, brownish-red color, as well as give the fish its characteristically pungent taste and smell. To find out how *red herring* came to be used figuratively, we need to turn to the early 1800s and to hunting or, more accurately, hunt saboteurs. The modern fox lover has a long history, for on hunt days the strong-smelling fish would be dragged by saboteurs along the hunt route and away from the fox. This confused the hounds, which followed the scent of the red herring rather than that of the fox, allowing it to scurry off to safety. So effective was this tactic that the expression soon passed into common usage.

Culinary Espionage à la Diamond Jim

Nicolas Marguery (1834–1910) was a culinary legend. His restaurant, Au Petit Marguery, was one of the most popular in Paris during the nineteenth century, the great and the good of French society regularly filling his dining room. In fact they still do, enjoying surroundings that have hardly changed since the famous chef was there, creating dish after dish in his busy kitchens, almost 150 years ago.

Nicolas Marguery's cooking, particularly his **sole Marguery**—sole served in a sauce of white wine and fish stock blended with egg yolks and butter (see also SOLE VÉRONIQUE)—was renowned throughout Europe and America. French cuisine was the world leader, and its chefs jealously guarded the recipes of their signature dishes. Sole Marguery was one such dish, and the story of how it emigrated from France to America is an intriguing one, full of subterfuge, audacity, and a level of commitment that is hard to imagine.

As the immigrants who introduced the HAMBURGER and the HOT DOG to New York settled throughout America, so the economy expanded, mainly through the growing railway network. Jim Brady (1856–1917), a salesman for the Manning,

Maxwell, and Moore Railroad Company, was part of this. And he was highly successful: the sums that he made selling railway tracks throughout America and across the world were so immense that he began to invest in diamonds and other precious stones, earning himself the nickname Diamond Jim.

A larger-than-life character, Brady also had a prodigious appetite. He was rumored to consume a gallon of orange juice, steak, potatoes, bread, flapjacks, muffins, eggs, and pork chops—just for breakfast. A mid-morning snack might be three dozen oysters and clams, followed by lunch of another three dozen oysters, three stuffed crabs, four lobsters, a joint of beef, and a salad. During the afternoon, Jim would down six sodas and a seafood snack before taking a nap, and then came dinner: thirty-six oysters, six lobsters, two bowls of green turtle soup, steak, vegetables, and a pastry platter. But it didn't end there: after a customary trip to the theater, where he would eat two pounds of candied fruit, Jim then rounded off his day with a supper of a half dozen game birds and a couple of large beers.

And this was Diamond Jim's intake every single day. His friend the restaurateur Charles Rector, owner of Rector's Restaurant on Broadway in New York, would import several barrels of extra-large oysters from Baltimore every day, just for Jim. It's hardly surprising, therefore, that Rector once described the railway magnate as "the best twenty-five customers I have ever had."

One afternoon, during a marathon eating session with friends, Diamond Jim began telling the group about the exquisite sole Marguery he had been served at Au Petit Marguery during a recent business trip to Paris. Unable to explain the recipe to Rector, he teased his friend that he might have to find another restaurant where he could eat sole

Marguery. Rector on the spot resolved to be the first restaurant in New York to serve the dish and set about obtaining the recipe, by fair means or foul. So he summoned his son, George, from Cornell University and sent him to Paris to obtain the recipe.

The young man arrived in Paris fully aware he could not walk into the restaurant as a complete unknown and ask for it, so he applied for a job as dish washer to see what he could learn from the kitchen staff. It soon became obvious that he would discover nothing from the chefs, who carefully guarded their recipes from all the menials in the kitchen, so George applied for a job as an apprentice chef.

It took him over two years of hard work to become senior enough to have the recipe for the legendary Marguery sauce explained to him, and as soon as it was he resigned, catching the boat back to New York. It is said that both his father and Diamond Jim Brady were waiting for him at the dockside as the ship drew in, with George shouting to them from the deck: "I got it!" The young chef was sent straight into the kitchen to prepare sole Marguery and, as legend has it, when Diamond Jim tasted the dish, he declared: "If you poured this sauce over a Turkish towel, I believe I could eat all of it!" And that, dear reader, is why the land of the free has a French-inspired dish going by the name of **sole Marguery à la Diamond Jim**.

Jim Brady died in his sleep in 1910 and only then did doctors discover he had an unusually large stomach, almost six times the size of a normal man's. George Rector went on to take over his father's restaurant business. He also wrote cookbooks and food columns for the newspapers, as well as hosted a radio show called *Dine with George Rector*. He is said to have literally dined out on the story of how he had claimed Marguery sauce for America for the rest of his life.

What Was the Inspiration for Sole Véronique?

Another classic dish made with sole (see also SOLE MARGUERY)—this time gently poached and served in a white-wine sauce to which seedless green grapes have been added—is **sole Véronique**. As with so many classic dishes, there is disagreement about who originally came up with it. Some say that it was the great chef Auguste Escoffier (see PEACH MELBA), who had accepted an invitation in 1890 from the impresario Richard D'Oyly Carte (1844–1901) to take over the kitchen of his new luxury hotel, the Savoy. D'Oyly Carte also ran the next-door Savoy Theater—subsequently celebrated for its staging of the operettas of Gilbert and Sullivan—and it was he who built the Royal English Opera House (now the Palace Theater), where the comic opera *La Basoche*, by French composer André Messager (1853–1929), was one of the first works to be put on. The opera went well, but it was Messager's *Véronique*, staged in London from 1898 and running for 496 performances, that took the capital by storm. It is said that, to mark the occasion of the opera's opening night, Escoffier created a dish in honor of the composer—a friend and fellow countryman—calling it sole Véronique.

Louis Diat, creator of VICHYSSOISE SOUP, had a different story, however. He believed that the inventor was one Monsieur Malley, a chef at the Paris Ritz (where Escoffier set up the kitchens in 1898). A special party was planned and Malley, in an imaginative twist to a classic dish, decided to add grapes to the sauce for the fish course. He gave instructions to a trusted under-chef and went out, as usual, for the afternoon. When he returned, he found the young man so excited that he could hardly work: his wife had just presented him with a baby girl, their first child. Monsieur Malley asked what they would name the child. "Véronique" came the reply.

"*Alors*," said the chef de cuisine, "we'll call the new dish *filets de sole Véronique*." And so it is called to this day.

Why Paella, Historically Speaking, Shouldn't Be in This Chapter

Today this archetypal Spanish dish is best eaten by the sea: its juicy yellow rice packed with shrimp and chunks of garlic cod, chicken, and chorizo. But **paella** was originally laborers' fare, cooked over an open fire in the fields of Valencia and eaten directly from the pan as a communal meal. The cooks used ingredients that were close at hand. Snails were the most commonly used meat, as they were easily scavenged; rabbit or duck would be added otherwise, and occasionally chicken. Even today, a paella made in the traditional Valencian style includes no seafood, although Valencians living by the sea—who would have used fish instead of meat—might beg to disagree.

The dish has a long history. Alan Davidson, in *The Penguin Companion to Food* (2002), describes it as symbolizing the union of two important cultures: the Roman, which gave us the special utensil in which it is cooked, and the Arab, which introduced that staple of Eastern cooking to Europe—rice. The name derives from the Latin word for a special kind of deep concave pan, *patella*—which is also, incidentally, the medical name for the kneecap (which does look quite like a pan resting face down). As time went on, the design of the patella/paella became flatter, adapting to the types of fires it was being cooked over. The Arabs (see GAZPACHO) traditionally cooked special communal dishes based on rice, often flavored with saffron, at family and religious feasts. (It was the Arab engineers' mastery of irrigation that meant rice could be grown much closer to Europe and led to it becoming a staple ingredient there.) Later, as rice became a much more common food, it was combined with beans and vegetables and dried cod, especially during Lent when meat was forbidden.

This was picked up on in Valencia where, from the eighteenth century, rice, flavored with saffron, was cooked in the open air in a paella pan. In the nineteenth century, with improvements in transport and general living standards, family outings to the countryside rapidly grew in popularity, and the making and eating of paella became an essential part of the fiesta. The dish soon caught on throughout Spain, with seafood being added to the original Valencian recipe, giving rise to seafood and mixed paella. Like GRAVLAX and BARBECUES, the cooking of paella has always been seen as a male activity, and there is even a special etiquette about eating from the communal pan: everyone takes his or her wooden spoon and draws a triangular wedge in the rice, marking it out in a kind of culinary round table.

The Salmon Dish That Returns
from the Grave

Gravlax or **gravad lax** is a popular Scandinavian dish commonly served as an appetizer as part of the traditional SMORGASBORD. Freshly caught salmon is skinned and boned, cut along its length and seasoned with salt, pepper, and sugar. One fillet is placed in a shallow bowl, skin side down, and seasoned with fresh dill, the second fillet laid on top, followed by a plate or board and a heavy weight. The salmon is then left in a cool place for three days or so. Every twelve hours, the fillets are turned and basted with the juices that have collected. In Scandinavia the making of gravlax is seen as a traditionally male activity (on a par with PAELLA or BARBECUE), stemming from the original, and rather unusual, way of preparing it.

Its earliest mention in print is from 1348, in the form of a name, Olafuer Gravlax, a man from Jämtland in Sweden. His surname, following a practice that was common at the time, indicated his profession—that is, he made the dish for a living, which suggests that gravlax must have already been in existence for some time. Fishermen like Olafuer would bone and fillet the salmon they caught, wrap it in birch bark and then bury it for 4–6 days in the brine-soaked sand just above the high-tide line. This short-term burial resulted in a fermentation that softened the flesh, giving it a tangy taste and rendering it edible while still essentially raw. The Scandinavian word for "hole in the ground," or "grave," is *grav*, while *lax* simply means "salmon." Although the dish is no longer prepared in this way, the name is still with us and "salmon from the grave" continues to haunt menus the world over.

Sushi: The Sour Dish That Became a Fast Food

It's a common fallacy to believe that **sushi** is always made with raw fish. This is to confuse the dish with SASHIMI, as rice is the main ingredient in sushi and the kind of fish traditionally used isn't raw but fermented. Every country with a coastline has come up with its own method of preserving freshly caught fish, whether salting, smoking, or pickling (see GRAVLAX). In Southeast Asia, cleaned, gutted, and salted fish were kept between layers of rice whose natural fermentation helped preserve it. In Japan this method was called *nare-zushi* (sushi or *zushi* translates as "it's sour"—from the taste of the vinegar produced by the fermenting rice); after a couple of months of fermentation, the rice was discarded and the fish was ready to eat. By the fourteenth century, the Japanese had started eating the rice alongside the fish in a dish called *seisei-sushi* that became extremely popular. The only downside was the delicacy's pungent smell, which has been described as a cross between blue cheese, fish, and rice vinegar, and so a quicker method of preserving the fish was devised, marinating it in rice vinegar alone.

How this turned into the version of the dish we are most familiar with today, **nigiri-sushi**, was down to one man, Yohei Hanaya, a grocer's son, born in 1799 deep in the Japanese countryside. When he moved to Tokyo in 1818, the only job he could find was working as a FAST FOOD vendor. Yohei was determined to be successful and struggled for some time to find the perfect recipe to appeal to the sophisticated palate of the people of Tokyo. Adapting the recipe for *seisei-sushi*, he used cooked rice in a vinegar dressing that he compressed into sticky, finger-shaped rolls (*nigiri* means "squeezed"), placing a slice of marinated fish on top of each one. Word soon spread of this new type of sushi that could be eaten with one's hands wherever and whenever one liked, and Yohei became very rich.

Why Sashimi Is Not for the Squeamish

A Japanese dish of raw fish, **sashimi** consists of slices of very fresh fish. The word comes from *sashi*, meaning "to pierce," and *mi*, "flesh." It's thought that this might derive from the traditional method of dispatching the fish, by piercing its brain with a sharp spike, killing it instantly. The fish is then placed immediately in ice, ensuring that it remains fresh for several days. In some restaurants in Japan a diner can choose their own sashimi from a tank full of live fish. The chosen fish is hooked out of the tank, carved into bite-size pieces, and eaten, all within the space of a few minutes. Traditionally sashimi is regarded as the most important part of a meal, hence only the best-quality fish is used, the type of fish depending on the season. Presented with great elegance, sashimi is often served on a bed of white radish with wasabi paste and soy sauce, although the dish has many variations.

8
Sauces and Seasonings

From Fine Sauces to Haute Cuisine:
The Evolution of French Cooking

Mayonnaise: The Sauce the British
Found Hard to Swallow

Kitchen Staple from the Thousand Islands

Pepper: The Black Gold of Former Times

How a Sprinkling of Salt Keeps the Devil at Bay

Béchamel: Return to the Mother Sauce

The United Nation of Mornay

Béarnaise: A Mother Sauce Begets a Child

The Accidental Birth of Beurre Blanc

Hollandaise: Sauce of the Huguenots

Worcestershire Sauce: Who Were
Mr. Lea and Mr. Perrins?

Does Horseradish Sauce Have Anything to
Do with Radishes, or Horses?

From Pickled Fish to Tomatoes: The Strange
Story of Ketchup

SAUCE, n. The one infallible sign of civilization and
enlightenment. A people with no sauces has one thousand vices; a people with one sauce has only nine hundred and ninety-nine. For every sauce invented and
accepted a vice is renounced and forgiven.

AMBROSE BIERCE, *The Devil's Dictionary*

From Fine Sauces to Haute Cuisine:
The Evolution of French Cooking

The word **sauce** is from Old French, based in turn on the Latin *salsus*, meaning "salted." In the days before refrigeration, meat, including fish and seafood, didn't stay fresh for long. Strong-tasting sauces were therefore used to mask the flavor, in much the same way as we'd put a throw over an ugly sofa. And they go back a long way in culinary history. The Romans, for instance, were obsessed by a potent fish sauce called "garum," made by crushing the intestines of various fish, including mackerel, tuna, and eel, and fermenting them in brine to produce a multipurpose condiment—a kind of precursor to WORCESTERSHIRE SAUCE. Like olive oil, the best garum was skimmed off the top of the rotting liquid and sold to the rich, while the dregs (called "allec") were snapped up by the poor to flavor their staple dish of PORRIDGE. Garum was also used as a medicine for many ailments, including dog bites (see also page 73), dysentery, and ulcers, and as a digestive aid to ease chronic diarrhea and to treat constipation. As time went by and cooking became more sophisticated, sauces became a more integral part of cooking. No longer just the culinary equivalent of throwing a blanket over an old sofa, they now blended with a dish. In the form of a marinade (see KEBAB), for instance, they tenderized meat, while as the liquid in a casserole or stew, they provided a liquor for the cooking, adding flavor and ensuring the other ingredients in the dish didn't dry out.

When Catherine de Médicis arrived at the French court in 1519, she was only fourteen years of age and wielded little influence. But when, in 1547, she finally became queen, she invited some of the finest chefs from her home town of Florence (see EGGS FLORENTINE), paving the way for a complete change in French cooking, for the chefs brought with them new ingredients and culinary techniques unknown outside Italy up until that point. Among the skills the Florentine chefs taught their hosts was how to uses spices and herbs to enhance a meal instead of disguising the taste, while butter and flour replaced stale bread as a thickening agent for stews.

Soon the French were surpassing their teachers, incorporating Italian techniques into an increasingly sophisticated cuisine of their own. Sauces took pride of place: split into five "mother" types on which all others were based (see BÉCHAMEL SAUCE for more on this), they laid the foundation for a whole range of new and subtle-flavored dishes. Food presentation also changed, with sweet and savory dishes being served as separate courses rather than together, and vegetables being presented as side dishes.

All this culminated, a century later, in a seminal cookbook, *Le Cuisinier françois*, written and published in 1651 by master chef François Pierre de la Varenne (1618–78) and one of the founding textbooks of modern French cuisine (see also SPANISH OMELET). It is clear, from the book, that by then chefs no longer favored strong spices—which had featured in upper-class cooking since the Middle Ages (see PEASE PUDDING)—replacing them in savory dishes with lighter, locally grown herbs, including parsley, tarragon, bay leaves, and sage. *Le Cuisinier françois* became an instant bestseller, its influence spreading beyond France to the rest of Europe, changing attitudes toward cooking and its presentation and providing recipes for many dishes, including sauces, that can be found on menus to this day.

Needless to say, it was only the upper echelons of society who benefited from such groundbreaking cuisine. The lower classes continued to live off much simpler fare, or, if they were a little less fortunate, they starved. Then, at the end of the eighteenth century, came that great event that rocked the whole of France, shaking up the lives of rich and poor alike—the French Revolution (see LOBSTER THERMIDOR). While the uprising was good news for the majority of the population, it clearly wasn't much fun for the nobility, for whom, thanks to Madame Guillotine, the finer points of dining etiquette were now no longer a priority. Nor was it much easier for anybody who had worked in the great chateaux and palaces, including the cooks and kitchen staff, who now had to look elsewhere for employment.

As a result, a number of them set themselves up in some of the many grand buildings of Paris that had been "liberated," in the hope that people would need feeding and be able to pay or barter for it. So began a different kind of revolution—a gastronomic one this time. Within a few years, these restaurants had become highly fashionable and full of an entirely new class of people, who were hooked on and prepared to pay for a sophisticated style of cooking previously accessible only to the nobility and known, therefore, as **haute** (high-class) **cuisine**.

How the Bloody French Revolution Changed Our Menus

The expression **à la carte** is a practical one used to describe fine dining when Parisian restaurants began to appear during and after the French Revolution. Prior to the revolution, the finest chefs in the world were usually employed by the French aristocracy and were exclusively tied to the kitchens of the great estates and palaces. After Napoleon had cut them down to size, many great cooks opened their own establishments and enjoyed the freedom the revolution had provided.

Prior to this, meals would only be taken communally and from a set menu, as coffeehouses and street vendors would only provide one meal and the hungry only had two choices, yes or no. (Which is still your only menu option on many budget airlines these days.) But the new Parisian restaurateurs were eager to display their skills and provided a menu offering diners a wide choice of specially prepared meals at varying prices from the **menu card**, which translates as "à la carte." The word "menu," evolved from the Latin *minutus*, meaning something small.

By contrast **table d'hote** describes a complete set meal of several courses for a fixed price and translates as "the table of the host." In other words, the restaurateur has chosen the menu for you, a particularly popular way of eating in large groups.

Mayonnaise: The Sauce the British Found Hard to Swallow

This famous cold white sauce, found in refrigerators the world over, is a simple mixture of olive oil, lemon juice or vinegar, and egg yolk. Its name may in fact derive from this last ingredient. According to *Larousse Gastronomique* (1961 edition), **mayonnaise** "is a popular corruption of *moyeunaise*, evolving from the Old French word *moyeu*, meaning egg yolk." Other theories abound, however, including one linked to Charles de Lorraine, Duke of Mayenne (1554–1611), who was so fond of a particular white sauce ("Mayennaise"), and spent so long eating a portion of chicken covered in it, that he lost the Battle of Arques in 1589 during the French

Wars of Religion. A far more likely reason is that he ran away after being confronted by four thousand British troops sent to reinforce British ranks facing the opposing French army.

I have also found references to an Irish general called Mac-Mahon, who claimed he first created the sauce, originally called "MacMahonnaise" (and presumably the ideal accompaniment for a Big Mac), and there are suggestions that it derives from "Bayonnaise" after the French city of Bayonne. However, it is far more likely that the now ubiquitous condiment originates from the town of Mahon, the capital of the Balearic Island of Minorca, and from an incident that reflects far less well on the British.

Minorca has been conquered several times throughout its history, most notably by the Carthaginian general Mago (243–203 BC), brother of Hannibal and legendary founder of Port Mahon, but in 1756 it was occupied by the British, who had become rather lazy about maintaining their defenses. The principal protection of the island was the responsibility of Admiral John Byng (1704–57) with his fleet of thirteen British ships. But due to a major tactical error, the fleet was decimated and the French were able to land fifteen thousand troops at Mahon under the leadership of the duc de Richelieu (1696–1788), a gentleman celebrated for his insistence on dining in the nude—which may well have led to his particularly enthusiastic championing of a new sauce that enhanced the flavor of cold foods (a much safer choice for the naked male diner) . . . but I'm getting ahead of myself here.

The British garrison of three thousand men surrendered the island to the French on May 28 and Byng returned to Gibraltar, where he was tried by court martial for incompetence and subsequently shot. Commenting on the trial in his satirical novella *Candide* (1759), French philosopher Voltaire famously wrote: "The British shoot an admiral every so often *pour encourager les autres* [to encourage the others]." Adding to British mortification, the invasion of Port Mahon on April 19 was so successful that the French didn't suffer a single fatality and Richelieu threw a lavish feast in celebration.

Legend has it that the duke's chef, when preparing the victory banquet, realized to his horror that he didn't have any cream to make the rich sauce he needed. In desperation he followed the recipe for a local sauce, **aioli**—popular in many Mediterranean countries—but omitted the industrial quantities of garlic essential to it. To his great relief, the result was a success; indeed, the duke liked it so much that he took the recipe back to France with him, calling it "Mahonnaise" in memory of his great victory over the British at Port Mahon. The use of mayonnaise as a dressing and as an ingredient for other sauces spread quickly throughout France following the duc de Richelieu's triumphant return to his homeland, where he dramatized and elaborated on the story of how the sauce was invented under his inspiration.

Kitchen Staple from the Thousand Islands

The exotically named Thousand Islands are a cluster of islands (there are 1,793 in total) in the Saint Lawrence River on the border between America and Canada. Every July and August, when New York turns into a humid oven, city dwellers traditionally escape to the islands, where many of the houses are owned by these vacationers. Around the turn of the twentieth century, a well-known Thousand Island fisherman, George LaLonde Junior, was teaching a prominent New York actress, May Irwin (1862–1938), to fish. One evening, following a fishing expedition, LaLonde's wife Sophia served one of her "shore dinners": the popular actress was particularly impressed with the salad dressing, made from mayonnaise and KETCHUP mixed with finally chopped green olives, pickles, onions, and hard-boiled eggs. Impressive as it was—and rather like the recipe concocted by the duc de Richelieu's chef (see MAYONNAISE)—the dressing was essentially made with whatever was at hand. On these islands at that time, with little access to fresh ingredients, dishes had to be prepared using pantry basics. May Irwin asked for the recipe and immediately passed it on to her friend and fellow Thousand Island vacationer George C. Boldt (1851–1916). Boldt, owner of the Waldorf Hotel in New York, was equally impressed with the sauce, asking his maître d,' Oscar Tschirky (see also EGGS BENEDICT and WALDORF SALAD), to refine it and introduce it to the diners at the hotel. Today **Thousand Island dressing** is internationally known and has itself become a supermarket basic, sold in bottles throughout the world.

Pepper: The Black Gold of Former Times

One of the oldest-known spices on the planet, **black pepper** has been used in flavoring for over seven thousand years. A much prized spice, it was frequently used for bartering instead of money. In AD 408, the Visigoths, a barbarian Germanic tribe led by Alaric the First, rebelled against the Romans. It was the first time in almost eight hundred years that the Romans had lost a major military conflict and the stakes were high. Alaric succeeded in pushing the Roman army back to Rome and then laid siege to the city. As winter approached, disease and starvation spread and the Senate, in desperation, tried to broker a deal, offering gold and black pepper in exchange for the liberation of the city. Alaric the First accepted the terms, thereby ensuring that pepper—at the time, equal in value to gold—would thereafter be known as the spice for which Rome, the heart of the greatest empire in history, had been traded.

Throughout the centuries that followed, pepper continued to be highly valued. The earliest reference to black peppercorns in England, for instance, can be found in the statute books of King Ethelred (978–1016) in which it is recorded that ships delivering to Billingsgate must pay a toll of a ten-pound sack of pepper at Easter and at Christmas. Peppercorns have a symbolic monetary value even today, enshrined in the English legal system. According to English law, every legal contract requires that each party gives something of value to the other. If not, then the contract is considered not to be binding and cannot be enforced. For example, when you sell your house, the other party gives you money for it, hence something of value is exchanged by each party, either a house or money. For the contract to be valid it is not necessary, however, for the items being exchanged to be equal in value, but an exchange must take place, even if something of very little value is offered in return for something of far greater worth. In such cases, a token sum may be given, historically measured in peppercorns. Hence a landlord wishing to let a property essentially for free must set up a contract with the leaseholder for a nominal sum, referred to as a *peppercorn rent*. Likewise, if a company has debts amounting to more than its overall worth, a new owner can obtain the business for no money at all, so long as they agree to take over the debt, but the contract between the two parties would not be legally binding if the buyer did not offer something nominal in exchange. This, by law, is known as a *peppercorn payment*. Obviously they use cash these days, but a single dollar payment is still known as the "peppercorn."

Pepper can also be regarded as a chief motivating factor in the Great Age of Discovery, which began during the late fifteenth century and continued into the early 1600s. European explorers, especially the Spanish and Portuguese, who were, by then, free of Moorish domination (see GAZPACHO), chartered ships to seek out new territories, establishing in the process trade links with previously unknown cultures. The shipping lanes between Europe and Asia soon became known as spice trade routes and for centuries black pepper was the principal commodity. During the mid-sixteenth century, for example, the price of pepper served as the basis for all European business at Antwerp in Belgium, in much the same way as the price of oil affects world trade today. Indeed, it was the passion for pepper, and the search for a new source of the valuable condiment (see CHILI PEPPER), that led to the King and Queen of Spain financing a certain voyage by one Christopher Columbus, who set out to find an old spice and instead discovered a new world.

How a Sprinkling of Salt Keeps the Devil at Bay

Salt is one of the most basic food seasonings. Before the introduction of the can and the refrigerator, it was also the chief means of preserving food and, like BLACK PEPPER, highly valued as a result (see also page 149). Its value was symbolic, too: the mineral was regarded as an auspicious substance by many religions and is still used in religious ceremonies today. In the Christian faith, holy water is said to derive from the ancient practice among the Egyptians, Greeks, and Romans of invoking the gods with offerings of salt and water. Meanwhile, the Bible frequently mentions salt, most famously in the reference to Lot's wife being turned into a pillar of salt for her disobedience, and in the words of Christ to his followers, whom he calls the "salt of the earth" (Matthew 5:13).

Numerous superstitions are associated with it as well.

During the Middle Ages, it was thought to neutralize the power of witchcraft. Anybody affected by a curse would be advised to sprinkle salt into an open fire every morning for nine consecutive days with the words: "Salt, salt, I drop thee into the fire and may the person who has bewitched me neither eat, drink, or sleep until the spell is broken." On the tenth morning, it was believed, the curse would be lifted. It was also believed that if a dead man's hand was placed on a plate of salt overnight, this would provide a cure for chilblains—providing you didn't mind having your feet rubbed by a salty, dead hand, that is. Belief in the curative powers of salt was so strong that it was thought that a bag of hot salt could cure toothache or earache and, if placed in a baby's crib, would protect an infant against illness and disease. In the north of England there is a legend claiming that during the Great Plague, which decimated London in 1665, every single employee of a former salt works escaped infection.

The most commonly known superstition connected with salt is that a person who spills it should take a pinch and throw it over their left shoulder. This was thought to blind the devil—lurking, it was believed, behind your left shoulder—so that he wouldn't notice the spillage and heap misfortune upon you. It's also why you should never stand behind a busy chef, unless you want to be showered with salt. The superstition appears to be religious in origin, dating back to the Last Supper when Jesus dined with his twelve Apostles and announced one of them would betray him to the Roman authorities. According to some accounts, Judas spilt a cellar of salt at the table and removed the offending mess by scooping it up and tossing it over his shoulder, a historic event said to have been depicted by Leonardo da Vinci in his painting *The Last Supper* (1498), although Judas must have disposed of the salt, as I can't see it anywhere.

As an auspicious, luck-bringing substance, salt was used as an early form of confetti, thrown over a newly wedded couple, or sprinkled on the ground after the bearer of bad news had left, to ensure he didn't return. It was also considered unlucky for a fisherman to set out to sea without a bag of salt in his boat. From ancient times until the Middle Ages, newborn babies were rubbed with salt to ward off evil spirits, a practice referred to in the Old Testament, in Ezekiel 15:8: "And as for thy nativity, in the day thou wast born thy navel was not cut, neither wast thou washed in water to supple thee; thou wast not salted at all." It was also used to mark the end of a person's life: in Wales, for instance, a plate of bread and salt would be placed on a coffin prior to burial, in the belief that the salt would soak up the dead person's sins. A local sin-eater would then consume the bread and salt, absolving the sins of the deceased and allowing them to rest in peace.

SALT features in many of our most common idioms. **Rubbing salt into the wound**, for instance, is to make a person's shame, or pain in an emotional sense, even worse than it already is. A frequently suggested source for the expression is nautical in origin. Once an errant sailor had been punished by flogging, his comrades would rub preserving salt into his wounds, making them much more painful but healing the injuries a good deal faster than if they had been left untreated. This may very well be the origin of the phrase, but for another possible source, and an earlier one at that, we need to turn to an associated idiom.

If someone is **not worth their salt**, they are regarded as not very good at their job or a particular task. During the days of the Roman Empire, salt was an expensive commodity and soldiers were paid partly in salt, which they carried with them in leather pouches. This form of payment was known as a *salarium*, from the Latin word *sal*, meaning "salt." Hence to be not worth one's salt would mean being not worth paying (in salt). It is thus easy to see how the English word **salary** also originates from the word *sal* (salt). Any Roman who had been injured in battle would have to rub part of his salt (i.e., his wages) into the wound to help the healing process.

Adding salt to food has given rise to another common idiom, **take with a grain of salt**. In the same way that a pinch of salt can make otherwise plain food more interesting and palatable, a metaphorical grain of salt will help us to accept something we are being told that we might otherwise doubt.

Béchamel: Return to the Mother Sauce

Béchamel, one of the five so-called mother sauces of French cuisine (the others being velouté, espagnole—both made using stock and thickened with flour and butter—HOLLANDAISE SAUCE, and tomato), is widely used in European and American cooking. A smooth, white sauce made with milk and thickened with flour and butter, béchamel is usually served with white meats, eggs, or vegetables. The question of its origin has long been the subject of debate, as noted by the New York food critic Raymond Solokov:

> Gastronomic literature is filled with tedious pages and trifling disputes and Béchamel has inspired more than its fair share of this piffle. People will argue about whether the correct spelling should not be *béchamelle* or if not the Italian version *balsamella* from the Romagna region is the original of the best known and easiest mother sauce. In such matters prejudice will always rule, for there is no evidence one way or the other. We

can only point to the appearance of a sauce called
Béchamel during the reign of Louis XIV of France.
And, as so often, the original sauce bore only a slight
resemblance to the modern version . . .

Following this lead, there was indeed a Marquis Louis de
Béchamel (1630–1703), a rich financier and a member of the
court of Louis XIV. In 1685, Béchamel took on the honorary
position of chief steward to the king. This was a position of
power, giving valuable access to the king, but it also entailed
great responsibility, ensuring that Louis XIV—a highly cultivated man, known as the "Sun King" for his sophistication and
love of culture—was happy with his food. The marquis is said
to have invented the sauce when trying to come up with a new
way of serving and eating dried cod. It is more likely to have
been created by one of the chefs who reported to Béchamel and
who dedicated it to him as a compliment or in return for a favor
after it was served to the king and became a royal favorite.

This prompted some jealousy along the way. The duc
d'Escars is recorded as commenting: "That fellow Béchamel
has all the luck. I was serving breast of chicken *à la crème* more
than twenty years before he was born, but I have never had the
honor of giving my name to even the most modest sauce."
You've probably never heard of the duc d'Escars either, which
is hardly surprising. As the great chef Auguste Escoffier (see
PEACH MELBA and SOLE VÉRONIQUE) correctly noted in his
memoirs: "After all, if it wasn't for his divine sauce the marquis de Béchamel would have been forgotten long ago." And
Escoffier wasn't often wrong when it came to food.

The United Nation of Mornay

A prime example of a mother sauce (see BÉCHAMEL) being used
as a base for something new is **Mornay sauce**. Many suggest

that this sauce—where two types of grated cheese, usually Gruyère and PARMESAN, are added to béchamel—was named after Philippe, duc de Mornay (1549–1623), a prominent French Protestant writer. But, as he predated Louis de Béchamel, de Mornay cannot have invented the sauce himself: it's far more likely that it was inspired by his life and achievements.

At the outbreak of the French Wars of Religion (1562–98) between the Catholics and the Protestants (known as Huguenots—see also HOLLANDAISE SAUCE), de Mornay joined the army, although a convenient fall from his horse meant that he avoided direct military action. Warned by a Catholic friend, he also managed to escape the St. Bartholomew's Day Massacre, a brutal campaign of mob violence and assassinations that took place in 1572 (see EGGS FLORENTINE). De Mornay spent the rest of his life devoting himself to furthering the Huguenot cause wherever possible, becoming known as one of its leading supporters, while his influence on European religion and politics is well documented. He was the right-hand man of the Protestant Henri de Navarre (see BÉARNAISE SAUCE), who converted to Catholicism for purely political reasons on gaining the French throne, declaring: "Paris is well worth a Mass." Once safely in power, however, he passed the Edict of Nantes, which, in recognizing Protestantism in France, marked the end of the Wars of Religion and restored peace to the nation. This sauce could be described as a microcosm of de Mornay's ideal France, with its two different, strong-tasting cheeses symbolizing the Protestants and Catholics living together in harmonious union.

Béarnaise: A Mother Sauce Begets a Child

And from the king's adviser (see MORNAY SAUCE) to the king himself . . . Henri IV (1553–1610), one of the few French kings to be granted the title of "Great," was a revolutionary monarch. Instead of waging costly wars to suppress opposing nobles, as all his predecessors had, Henri simply paid them off. He is often quoted as saying: "If God spares me, I will ensure that there is no working man in my kingdom who does not have the means to have a chicken in the pot every Sunday!" An attitude that was highly unusual for someone of his standing, demonstrating how well he understood the plight of the French worker or peasant farmer. Never before had a French ruler really considered the welfare of his subjects, nor would one again until the French Revolution. Meanwhile, the peace that Henri restored to France following decades of religious war ushered in a period of relative prosperity that would have helped put a chicken in every peasant's pot.

After he was stabbed by a Catholic fanatic, the French people mourned their monarch, whom they had nicknamed Le Béarnais after his birthplace, Béarn, a former province in the Pyrenees in southwest France. Statues were raised, portraits painted, and books written in honor of Le Béarnais. But the sauce that bears his name wasn't invented until the nineteenth century when chef Jules Colette, working at a restaurant named after the king, Le Pavillon Henri IV, invented his own, extremely delicious version of HOLLANDAISE SAUCE. **Béarnaise sauce**—an emulsion of egg yolks and clarified butter, flavored with herbs—rapidly became as popular as its royal namesake, so much so that every chef at the smart Parisian restaurant tried to claim it as their own.

The Accidental Birth of Beurre Blanc

Another famous sauce, **beurre blanc** ("white butter") apparently evolved from a mistake made by French chef Madame

Clémence Lefeuvre toward the end of the nineteenth century while she was working in the kitchens of the marquis de Goulaine. On one occasion, the story goes, intending to make BÉARNAISE SAUCE for a pike dish, Lefeuvre ran out of eggs at the crucial moment and had to quickly improvise, using wine and lemon juice instead. Legend has it that her new sauce became so popular she opened her own restaurant, La Buvette de la Marine, on the banks of the Loire River near Nantes, on the strength of it with beurre blanc as her signature sauce.

Hollandaise: Sauce of the Huguenots

An emulsion of egg yolk and butter, seasoned with lemon juice, **hollandaise sauce** would appear, from its name, to come from Holland, but the recipe is not an obviously Dutch one. Like so many other dishes, it has a strong connection to the French Huguenots (see also BÉARNAISE SAUCE and EGGS FLORENTINE), a Protestant minority in a country dominated by the Catholic Church. Subjected to religious persecution from the sixteenth century, they were forced to emigrate, and by the end of the seventeenth century—when Louis XIV revoked the Edict of Nantes (see MORNAY SAUCE)—roughly two hundred thousand Huguenots had been driven from France. They sought refuge in the Protestant countries of northern Europe, including England, Germany, and the Netherlands, gradually returning to France when it was safe to do so. Huguenots returning from Holland brought back with them a sauce that they had developed during their time away. Very like MAYONNAISE, it was made using melted butter rather than olive oil, which would have been difficult to obtain so far north.

Hollandaise is thought to have been originally called **sauce Isigny**, after the butter-producing town of Isigny-sur-Mer in Normandy, the butter and cream capital of France. When butter production ceased in the region during World War I, a new source had to be found, and so it was imported from Holland. Hence it was from around this time, according to one theory, that sauce Isigny became known as hollandaise sauce. Which sounds a little unlikely, however, as the Dutch association with the sauce had been established well before then. There is, for instance, a recipe for *sauce à la hollandoise* in the 1758 edition of François Marin's *Les Dons de Cormus*. Likewise, Mrs. Beeton, in her *Book of Household Management* (1861), refers to a "Dutch sauce, for fish," as well as a variant, "Green sauce, or Hollandaise verte." Probably both names, hollandaise and sauce Isigny, existed side by side until the former eventually won through as the name familiar to cooks the world over.

Worcestershire Sauce: Who Were Mr. Lea and Mr. Perrins?

In the 1830s, in the cellar below a chemist's shop in Worcester, England, called Lea & Perrins, a barrel of spiced vinegar—made according to an Indian recipe for a customer but never collected as it had been considered undrinkable— sat for some years. Clearing out the cellar, the chemists were about to throw away the barrel but fortunately tasted it first, finding, to their astonishment, that the mixture had nicely matured. And so **Worcestershire sauce** was born. The exact ingredients of the recipe are jealously guarded, but they include soy sauce and anchovies, which is why the mixture started fermenting. Worcestershire sauce is thus a modern, and rather more palatable, version of the Roman fish sauce **garum** (see "From Fine Sauces to Haute Cuisine," page 139). In 1838, the first distinctively labeled bottles of "Lea & Perrins Worcestershire Sauce" were released to the general public, and Mr. Lea and Mr. Perrins subsequently made their fortune from the distinctive-tasting condiment. The sauce remains hugely popular around the world to this day, especially in China and Japan, where it is praised for enhancing *umami*—the fifth basic taste, or "savoriness," considered fundamental to their cuisine.

Does Horseradish Sauce Have Anything to Do with Radishes, or Horses?

Many people wouldn't eat their roast beef without a good dollop of this fiery condiment made from grated horseradish root, mixed with cream and vinegar. The first reference to the plant was made by Roman scholar Pliny the Elder (AD 23–79) in his *Natural History*, published in AD 77–79, where he recommended it for its medicinal qualities; indeed, the roots and leaves of the plant were still used for this purpose during the Middle Ages. While it belongs to the same family of Asian plants, also including mustard, broccoli, and cabbage, horseradish is not actually a radish, although the name may have arisen because people regarded it as a hotter, coarser version of the smaller plant. Equally, the name may relate to the old European method of processing the vegetable by crushing it under a horse's hoof. More likely is the suggestion that it arose as a mistranslation of the German term *Meerrettich* as "mare radish." The correct translation would be "sea radish," reflecting how the plant grows wild in coastal areas. So the only horses there would be the proverbial white ones crashing on the beach nearby.

From Pickled Fish to Tomatoes: The Strange Story of Ketchup

Ketchup, as a condiment, far predates the sauce in the form we know it today. For centuries, the Chinese have been enjoying a spicy, pickled fish sauce made with anchovies, walnuts, mushrooms, and kidney beans, and known as *ke-tsiap.* The Indonesians made their own version, which they called *kecap.* Seventeenth-century British seamen brought *kecap* home with them and it rapidly caught on, the word evolving, Chinese whisper fashion, into "catchup" and then, by 1711, into "ketchup." The first ketchup recipe, printed in 1727 in Eliza Smith's *Compleat Housewife*, called for anchovies, shallots, vinegar, white wine, sweet spices (including cloves, ginger, mace, and nutmeg), BLACK PEPPER, and lemon peel. At this point, it was still a fish-based sauce, therefore, not unlike WORCESTERSHIRE SAUCE.

It was the Americans who introduced the tomato to the sauce, the first recipe for **tomato ketchup** being published in 1801 by Sandy Addison. In 1837, Americans selling tomato ketchup in Britain were encouraged to rename it "tomato chutney" in order to draw attention to the difference between their product and the mushroom ketchup popular there. Then the American ketchup boom happened, and the British mushroom ketchup was left behind in the rush: by 1900, there were over a hundred manufacturers of ketchup in the United States. But when Henry Heinz (see also BAKED BEANS) added tomato ketchup to his line of pickled products in 1872, his recipe became and remains the market leader. A large part of its initial success lay in its cunning advertising, pointing out that Heinz ketchup could free the family cooks from the laborious tyranny of making their own tomato sauce: "Blessed relief for Mother and the other women in the household!"

9
The Meat Course

What Are the Origins of the Sunday Roast?

Where Do the Noble Names for Beef Come From?

The Dark Story Behind Steak Diane

Favorite Dish of the Iron Duke

Frozen Food from Siberia: How Beef Stroganoff
Came About

Haggis: A Covert Symbol of Rebellion?

The Stew Wars of the Good Ol' Deep South

Irish Stew and Its Cousins Across the Sea

Was Steak Tartare the Original Food on the Hoof?

The Great Italian Soprano Banned by Immigration,
and It Wasn't the Gangster!

Why Chicken Kiev Rules Supreme

Possibly the First Curry Ever to Reach New York City

Bangers and Mash: Exploding Food
from the Trenches

How Goulash Helped Overthrow Oppression

How Does Meat Become Jerky?

What Is the Difference Between Shepherd's
and Cottage Pie?

Man is a carnivorous production,
And must have meals, at least one meal a day;
He cannot live, like woodcocks, upon suction,
But, like the shark and tiger, must have prey;
Although his anatomical construction
Bears vegetables, in a grumbling way,
Your labouring people think beyond all question,
Beef, veal, and mutton better for digestion.

LORD BYRON, *Don Juan*

What Are the Origins of the Sunday Roast?

On March 7, 321, the Emperor Constantine (c. 272–337), a convert to Christianity, passed the first law marking out Sunday as a day of rest: "On the venerable Day of the Sun let the magistrates and people residing in cities rest, and let all workshops be closed." As Christianity became an integral part of Western life—indeed, it was under Constantine's rule that it became the dominant religion in the Roman Empire—more rules were passed, banning all kinds of activities on Sunday, except, of course, eating. Sunday was a special day, the one day off in the week for working people, and the main meal should be special, too. Everyone was expected to attend church on a Sunday morning and the slap-up meal they enjoyed on their return home—often the one meal of the week where they ate meat—was a reward for behaving so virtuously. During the Middle Ages, the lord of the manor would provide a roast ox for his serfs, thus initiating the tradition of the **Sunday roast**.

It wasn't until the twentieth century that it was common for every home to have its own oven. Prior to that, the poorer families of the parish often stopped off at bakeries on their way to church and placed joints of meat in the large bread ovens that were still cooling down from Saturday night's baking. They could then pick up the meat, roasted to perfection, on their way home.

Where Do the Noble Names
for Beef Come From?

SIRLOIN

Taken from the rear back portion of the animal, **sirloin** is one of the most prized cuts of beef. According to folklore, Henry VIII (1491–1547), renowned for his love of food and drink, once so enjoyed a loin of beef that he bestowed a knighthood upon it. And so, much to the great amusement of his court, the favored cut became known thereafter as Sir Loin. I would love that story to be true, but, sadly, it is far more likely that the term is Old French in origin, from *surlonge*, meaning "above the loin." The sirloin is, after all, the "upper" cut of the loin of beef.

CHATEAUBRIAND

A **chateaubriand**, a thick cut of tenderloin steak that is usually broiled or grilled, is also French in origin, named in honor of the celebrated writer François-René de Chateaubriand (1768–1848). Oppressed by his gloomy, slave-trading father, Chateaubriand didn't get off to a happy start in life, the only relief being provided by long country walks with his sister Lucile, with whom he had an unnaturally close relationship. At seventeen, he left to join the army and in two years was promoted to captain, but a year later, in 1788, he suddenly lost interest in his military career after meeting several leading French authors. When the French Revolution broke out, Chateaubriand was so appalled at the violence he saw in Paris that he left for America, where he settled in the Deep South in 1791.

He had all kinds of adventures there, later claiming to have lived with Native American Indian tribes, an experience that inspired his third published work, *René* (1802), a painful, strangely familiar-sounding, tale of an unhappy Frenchman living with the Natchez tribe of Louisiana after fleeing an intense, possibly incestuous, relationship with his sister Amélie. *René* was an immediate success, cited as a major influence on the group of poets, painters, and writers of what would later become known as the Romantic Movement. These included the likes of Percy Bysshe Shelley and Lord Byron, who became as famous for their fussy ruffled shirts as they did for their work. If these artists regarded Chateaubriand as the father of Romanticism, then that must make him the grandfather of New Romanticism and the rash of frilly-shirted, floppy-haired pop bands that burst forth in the early 1980s.

Chateaubriand returned home from America following an amnesty issued by Napoleon to all those who had fled France during the Revolution, and secured his fame with his next book, *The Genius of Christianity*, published in 1802. This took the form of an apology for the Christian faith and the part it had played, or not played as the case may be, in the Revolution. Napoleon, who was keen to appease the Catholic Church, heartily approved and soon appointed the writer as secretary of the legation to the Holy See (the Vatican), and Chateaubriand embarked on a long career as a writer and politician, rising to the role of state minister in 1815.

However, his refusal to swear an allegiance to King Louis-Philippe in 1830 ended his political career and Chateaubriand spent the rest of his life writing controversially about the new monarch, disparaged as the "bourgeois king," and other sensitive issues of the day. While his influence as a writer continued to grow—a young Victor Hugo once wrote, "to be Chateaubriand or nothing"—his fans were not just literary ones. It is reputedly while he was serving as French ambassador to London in 1822 that his chef, Montmireil, famously christened a dish—beef tenderloin served in a sauce of white wine, shallots, and tarragon—after his adored master. Although

When you are given the **cold shoulder**, it is obvious you are not welcome anymore. Like "humble pie" (see page 237), this phrase can be traced back to the great banquets of medieval England. During the feasts, which could last for days, lavish dishes were washed down with lashings of wine and ale, while traveling musicians, dancers, and jesters entertained the guests. But all good things have to come to an end, and it was customary for the host to conclude the festivities by asking his cooks to serve slices from shoulders of cold beef, mutton, or pork. It was useful shorthand for the host to send the message in this way rather than to visit all his many guests in person to inform them the party was over. This tradition then passed to lower-class meals, where the host would serve guests who had outstayed their welcome from a *cold shoulder* of mutton. These days to be "given the cold shoulder" is perceived as unkind treatment, although in medieval times it was regarded as a civilized and polite gesture.

more often served with BÉARNAISE SAUCE today, chateaubriand steak continues to be enjoyed as it has been, by Romantics old and new, for some two hundred years.

The Dark Story Behind Steak Diane

Diana ("Diane" to the French) was the Roman goddess of virginity and the moon. She was also goddess of the hunt, and since Roman times certain game dishes have been dedicated to her. In France, joints of venison *à la Diane* were sautéed and

served with a sharp-tasting sauce to complement the sweet-
ness of the meat. The earliest mention of **sauce Diane** in
print wasn't until the twentieth century, however, when a recipe for it appeared in *Le Guide culinaire* by Auguste Escoffier
in 1907 (see also PEACH MELBA and SOLE VÉRONIQUE). Described
as a *sauce poivrade* (pepper sauce), this was finished with
whipped cream and pieces of hard-boiled egg white and truffle
cut in small crescent shapes in honor of the goddess.

After World War II, when thousands of American GIs
returned home after being stationed in France, **steak Diane**
(as the dish was called by then, although consisting of beef
rather than venison and served with a different sauce) began
to find its way onto the menus of many big city restaurants. In
New York during the 1950s and 1960s, a number of top hotels
created versions of steak Diane as their signature dish, each
claiming to have invented it. None of them had, of course, but
they all had their own unique variations. Further afield, at the
Copacabana Palace Hotel in Rio de Janeiro, Brazil, presenting the dish was made into a theatrical spectacle. The steak
was hammered until it was very thin and then, on a small gas
burner by the diner's table, quickly fried in butter, brandy
poured over, and the pan flamboyantly set aflame. The table-
side chef, presumably wearing a fireproof hat, would then fin-
ish the sauce with more butter, chives, and a splash of sherry.

But there is a more macabre aspect to this dish, one that
diners would probably prefer not to contemplate as they cut
into their juicy steaks. As goddess of the hunt, Diana was a
popular subject for painters from the Renaissance onward.
According to Roman myth—and in a scene famously painted
by the great Venetian artist Titian (c. 1488–1576)—Actaeon,
out hunting in the forest, accidentally came across Diana
while she was bathing in a secluded pool. As no mortal was
allowed to see her naked, the furious goddess immediately
turned him into a stag in punishment. The hunter became

the hunted and when his own pack of hounds caught up with him, they tore him apart and ate him. Hence mythologically speaking, at least, Actaeon was the original steak Diane.

Favorite Dish of the Iron Duke

The Iron Duke, who beat Napoleon at the Battle of Waterloo, was the British hero who has given his name to a range of items, including numerous streets and pubs, and a truly delicious way of cooking beef fillet in pastry.

Arthur Wellesley, 1st Duke of Wellington (1769–1852), was a brilliant and daring soldier who pursued successful military campaigns in India, Spain, Belgium, and the Netherlands. He was happiest enjoying a Spartan existence, staying in tents alongside his soldiers. He was so indifferent to what he ate—food was just fuel—and the cooking conditions were so basic, that he had a very high turnover of chefs. But then, according to the legend, one chef came up with the duke's ideal dish: one that he then insisted on serving at every formal dinner he was to hold for the rest of his long life.

It was the fashion at the time to bake joints of meat in pastry so they would remain moist. Like his men, Wellington preferred beef to any other meat, and to add extra flavor, his cook added a creamy mushroom paste to the fillet before wrapping it in pastry. The resulting dish was tender and delicious: the duke approved, the chef felt appreciated, and the recipe for **beef Wellington** was soon picked up by keen cooks all over the world.

Apart from the French, that is, who cannot bring themselves to honor the man who crushed their little leader at Waterloo in 1815: their version of the dish has added truffles and pâté de FOIE GRAS and simply is known as *filet de boeuf en croûte*. Indeed, an alternative theory is that during the Napoleonic Wars, when England was constantly at odds with France, a patriotic British chef changed the title of what was basically a French dish in order to give it an English name, one honoring the man who would decimate their enemy. Yet another theory suggests that the dish, wrapped in well-browned pastry, so resembled one of Wellington's long military boots that it was named after the celebrated wearer of them.

Frozen Food from Siberia: How Beef Stroganoff Came About

It will surprise few people to learn that **beef stroganoff**, a favorite winter dish, was developed deep in the Siberian Plains of Russia. Created by sautéing thinly sliced pieces of beef with onions, mushrooms, and paprika and then stirring in sour cream, the dish is credited to the chef of one of Russia's most colorful families of its imperial past, the Stroganovs. Unlike the egalitarian French, who tended to name a dish after the man who created it, regardless of his status, the Russian dynasties usually took the credit if one of their kitchen workers made a success of a new idea.

The Stroganov in question credited with the dish bearing his family name is Count Paul Sergeyevich (1823–1911), a prominent nineteenth-century Russian diplomat, well known across Europe and a close confidant of the Tsar. But it turns out that he was taking credit for a dish invented for one of his ancestors, another Paul Stroganov, Pavel (Paul) Alexandrovich (1772–1817)—a diplomat, like his descendant, and a lieutenant-general serving in the Napoleonic Wars between 1811 and 1815.

Legend has it that when his infantry battalion was stationed in the bleak Siberian wastelands, his chef discovered that their solidly frozen meat ration was easier to cope with when it had been cut up and then stored in thin strips, rather than larger cuts that needed to be thawed properly before they could be cooked. Other ingredients available in the wilderness out there were wild mushrooms and onions, presumably plenty of SALT and as much milk, or cream, as they could squeeze out of the local cows and goats. The recipe for the subsequent creation soon became a family favorite and was popularized by successive Stroganovs, including the younger Count Paul.

Beef stroganoff became fashionable in England when the recipe was first published in Ambrose Heath's *Good Food* in 1932, and it traveled across the water to America when GIs returning after World War II took home with them Count Stroganov's dish of sautéed beef, served Siberian-style.

Haggis: A Covert Symbol of Rebellion?

No book about food would be complete without this great Scottish favorite. The original recipe for **haggis** consists of the heart, lungs, and liver of a sheep minced with onion, oatmeal, and suet, stuffed into the animal's stomach lining and simmered for three hours. And when served with mashed potatoes and turnips, or tatties and neeps as gastronomes in Scotland call them, it becomes their national dish.

Some believe haggis first arrived in Scotland with the Vikings around AD 800 and that the word itself evolved from the Old Norse *haggva*, which loosely translates as "to chop up," although the idea of serving an animal's entrails, or offal, wrapped in its stomach lining or intestines was hardly unique to the Vikings or the people they invaded. It's essentially how sausages are made (see BANGERS AND MASH), after all. Nose-to-tail eating was a pragmatic product of the hand-to-mouth existence of life in the past: nothing edible could be wasted. The French have a similar dish, **andouillette**, originally served for the coronation of Louis II at Troyes in September 878, and, delving further back in time, the Romans were known to have made a haggis-like dish of animal intestines stuffed with entrails. There is even a section in Homer's *Odyssey* (c. 800 BC) comparing its hero, Odysseus, to someone roasting a "stomach full of fat and blood" over a blazing fire.

There is, however, very little evidence that the offal pudding called haggis is purely Scottish in origin. The first known written recipe for "hegese," as it was termed, is in a Lancashire cookbook, *Liber Cure Cocorum* ("The Art of Cookery"), dating from around 1430. It was certainly a common English food during the early seventeenth century, as Gervase Markham noted in his 1615 cookbook *The English Housewife*: "Oatmeal mixed with blood and the liver of either sheep, calf, or swine, makes the pudding called a haggas or haggus, of whose goodness it is in vain to boast because there is hardly to be found a man that does not affect them."

What is more interesting is why the Scots proudly claim haggis as their national dish: it's linked with their favorite poet, Robert Burns (1759–96). The son of a Scottish farmer, Burns began writing poetry as a teenager. His early works (written in Scottish dialect) were dedicated to various local beauties, and his roving eye led to an increasingly bad reputation, which was only compounded when two local girls became pregnant. The young farm laborer was under great financial stress with no means to support a single family, never mind two. On November 27, 1786, he set out for Edinburgh, with his manuscripts under his arm, principally to find out if he had anything worth publishing.

When his collection was bought and published to great critical acclaim, the young man instantly became part of the Edinburgh social elite, accepting invitations from academics, writers, artists, and aristocrats. Consequently, Robert Burns's lifestyle varied little until his death at the age of thirty-seven in 1796, still dominated by his preoccupation with women, to whom he dedicated much of his poetry. He also knew how to enjoy a party: his poem "Auld Lang Syne" is still sung all round the world at midnight on New Year's Eve, despite the fact that only a tiny fraction of those singing it, even in Scotland, have a clue what the words mean. Such is his importance as a poet that the anniversary of his birth is celebrated on January 25 every year by Scots around the world.

The format of Burns Night has become a tradition. The centerpiece consists of a vast haggis that is brought in, to the wailing of bagpipes, and toasted with Scotch whisky by all there, while Burns's "Address to a Haggis" is read out. It's a comic poem that lists the many virtues of haggis, insisting how wrong so-called sophisticates are to look down on it, as it's the true food of Scotland and properly sustaining, unlike fancy foreign dishes, which would make even a pig sick. But behind the humor is a serious purpose. Burns was writing shortly after the failure of the Jacobite Risings (1688–1746) against the English, who had in punishment stamped down on all things Scottish (the wearing of tartan, for instance, was punishable by seven years in prison). To Burns and his Scottish followers, it was crucial to celebrate all the aspects of Scottish life and culture in case they ceased to exist altogether. Because Burns wrote in a strong dialect that was opaque to non-Scots, his English readers missed the openly rebellious message of "Address to a Haggis." Here's a translation of one of the verses:

But take note of the strong haggis-fed Scot,
The trembling earth resounds his tread.
Clasped in his large fist a blade,
He'll make it whistle;
And legs and arms and heads he will cut off,
Like the tops of thistles.

Note to American readers: ignore what the Scots tell you; haggis is not a small furry animal that lives in the Highlands and has one set of legs that are shorter than the other, enabling it to run nimbly along the steep slopes of the Scottish mountains.

The Stew Wars of the Good Ol' Deep South

The town of Brunswick, Georgia, claims to be the home of the original **Brunswick stew** recipe, and a twenty-five-gallon cast-iron pot on a concrete pillar at the entrance to town bears a plaque confidently stating its claim. Arguably the most popular stew in America, it was first cooked in that very pot in 1898. However, local legend in Brunswick County, Virginia, insists that "Uncle" Jimmy Mathews, an African American hunting camp cook, created a squirrel stew for his employer, Creed Haskins, while on a hunt in 1828 along the banks of the Nottoway River. The Virginia General Assembly issued a proclamation in 1988 supporting their county's claim to be the "original home of Brunswick stew." Haskins, a member of the Virginia State Legislature, had been hunting all day with a group of friends while Uncle Jimmy slow-cooked the squirrels with butter, onions, corn, and stale bread, and the result proved to be so popular Haskins began ordering it to be served at political rallies, fund-raising events, and church functions throughout the state of Virginia, although the original squirrel meat was soon replaced with chicken.

Brunswick stew was soon such a favorite dish among the good ol' boys of the Deep South that stew makers from all over Virginia County now attend the annual Brunswick Stew Festival held at the 17th Street Farmers' Market in Richmond. Chefs compete for the honor of creating the best version in the state, a tradition taken very seriously around those parts—just ask the Brunswick Stewmaster's Association. In light of this documented evidence linking Brunswick stew to Creed Haskins, the town of Brunswick has not given up without a fight. The Brunswick Rockin' Stewbilee is held in October every year, and during the 1980s challenged the Brunswick County stew chefs to a cook-off, which started the Stew Wars featured in *Southern Living* magazine. And no, I am not making this up.

Irish Stew and Its Cousins Across the Sea

Irish stew, celebrated as the national dish of Ireland, should be made just with neck of mutton (mature sheep), potatoes, onions, and water, according to purists. In Ireland, only the older sheep were eaten, as the younger animals, although more tender, were too useful as a source of milk and wool. For the non-purist, additional ingredients might include carrots, turnips, and pearl barley, or, when circumstances were dire, pretty much anything available. The genius of the recipe is that its slow cooking is the perfect way to make the tough joints of mutton tasty and delicious. Traditionally, Irish stew would have been cooked for many hours over an open fire. Its status as a national dish, and a filling one at that, has been acknowledged for centuries, as exemplified by these lines from an English broadsheet ballad from around

1800: "Then hurray for an Irish Stew/That will stick to your belly like glue."

But Irish stew is not unique. Over the sea, in Britain, various regions have a similar dish. **Scotch broth**, for instance, uses lamb or mutton, pearl barley, carrots, and turnips. **Lancashire hotpot** is essentially the same: lamb or mutton and potatoes all cooked together, very slowly, in a large pot. In the port of Liverpool, famous for having many Irish immigrants, a similar dish, called *lapskaus*—the Norwegian word for "stew"—was imported by Scandinavian sailors during the eighteenth century. The name of the dish was corrupted to "lobs course," "lobscouse," and finally **scouse**, the word—like other diet-based national nicknames, such as Limey and Kraut (see SAUERKRAUT)—becoming associated with the good folk of Liverpool. A "pan of scouse" became a common part of the diet in working-class areas of the city, while **blind scouse** is the version made without meat. Made with lamb or mutton, onions, carrots, and as many potatoes as will fit in the pot, the dish is cooked slowly, to tenderize cheap cuts of meat, just like its more celebrated cousin, the traditional Irish stew.

Was Steak Tartare the Original Food on the Hoof?

Steak tartare is made from minced, ground, or finely chopped meat—chiefly beef but also venison and, in some countries, horsemeat. Sometimes it is cut into strips and beaten until flat, then marinated, chilled, and served raw, often with an equally raw egg yolk on top. It's most likely that the dish gets its name from **tartare sauce**—made with MAYONNAISE mixed with finely chopped onions, cucumber, and capers—served with steak in French restaurants early in the twentieth century. Originally called *steak à l'américaine*, the recipe then evolved into the dish as we know it today.

There is, however, a much more entertaining suggestion for its origin: that the dish comes from the Tartars themselves—the nomadic people of the Central Asian steppes. Renowned horsemen, their name, Tatar or Tartar, derives from the Turkish or Persian *Tätär*, meaning a mounted courier or messenger, although some etymologists maintain that the "r" was added by the Romans, who associated the savage riders with Tartarus, their name for Hell.

Fiercest among the Tartars was their famed leader, the emperor of all emperors, Genghis Khan (c. 1167–1227), who invaded and conquered two-thirds of the known world—stretching from the Pacific to the River Volga—with his army of Mongol horsemen. Constantly on the move, his men had to eat on the hoof—quite literally. Famous for staying in their saddles for very long periods as they rode toward yet another land in need of conquering, the Mongols discovered that if they carried their meat ration wedged under their saddles, by the end of the day the toughest piece of steak would be tenderized enough to eat. Sometimes they would chop up and flatten this meat into little patties, which tasted better warm off the horse's flank than if the rider had stopped to build a camp fire to cook his food.

By the time the emperor's grandson, Khublai Khan (1215–94), finally conquered Moscow, they had introduced their tenderized meat rations to the locals, who named it steak Tartar, which, for them, meant "steak of the violent invaders." Over the years, chefs from Russia and farther afield developed the dish, and diners no longer need to ride over rugged terrain for several days with it wrapped around their horses before eating it.

It's a great story, but according to some historians, there's no reference to such a practice in medieval records, neither in the Middle or the Far East. Their theory is that the story most likely arose from an existing practice by the Central Asian nomads for putting pieces of meat on their horses' backs. But the reason they did it was to lubricate and soothe their mounts' sores, much as we would put a raw steak on a black eye. Which isn't to say that they wouldn't have eaten it afterward.

The Great Italian Soprano Banned by Immigration, and It Wasn't the Gangster!

Another hugely popular dish from San Francisco (see CEL-ERY VICTOR), **Tetrazzini** can be made with either chicken or tuna with mushrooms and PARMESAN and is usually served on a nest of SPAGHETTI.

Over the road from the St. Francis Hotel stands the imposing Palace Hotel that was destroyed by fire after the great San Francisco earthquake of 1906. Having been completely rebuilt in 1909, the Palace Hotel became home to the great Italian soprano singer Luisa Tetrazzini (1871–1940), who had made her American debut in San Francisco in 1905 for the Metropolitan Opera Association. The singer's short stay in San Francisco was such a success that she was immediately taken to New York by the famous theatrical impresario Oscar Hammerstein only to find immigration complications preventing her from performing anywhere in the United States, frustrating both singer and agent. Tetrazzini eventually held a press conference and famously announced, "I will sing in San Francisco even if I have to sing in the street, because I know the streets of San Francisco are free": a line that would later become as famous as the singer herself.

Eventually Tetrazzini and Hammerstein won their legal battle, and on Christmas Eve 1910, the Italian soprano walked onto the stage near Lotta's Fountain on Market Street in San

Francisco and serenaded more than three hundred thousand people. Tetrazzini eventually performed in New York for Hammerstein's Manhattan Opera Company in 1911 and for the Boston and Chicago opera companies between 1911 and 1914 before returning to London and competing with her great rival Nellie Melba (see PEACH MELBA) for attention at the Royal Opera House. Along her travels Luisa Tetrazzini met novelist E. M. Forster, who featured the singer as a fat, sweating Italian lady who insisted on keeping the window open during a cold train journey in his first book, *Where Angels Fear to Tread*, which was first published in 1905 and inspired by Forster's travels with his mother. Forster was clearly no fan of Luisa Tetrazzini, although fortunately Ernest Arbogast was, as he was the chef at the Palace Hotel in San Francisco during the singer's stay and invented the popular **Tetrazzini sauce** in honor of her Christmas Eve performance in the city.

Why Chicken Kiev Rules Supreme

Possibly the most famous chicken recipe in the world, what we know as **chicken Kiev** was originally an Italian dish called *pollo sorpresa*, or "chicken surprise." The surprise is the molten garlic butter that jets out of the breadcrumb-covered chicken breast once you stick a fork in it. The French version of this—acknowledging the fact that the whole point of a surprise is that you don't know it's coming—is known as *suprême de volaille*, "best chicken" (although it can also refer to chicken breast cooked in a rich white sauce). It was the French version that gave the world the taste for the dish, and it was all due to Napoleon (1769–1821). A keen military campaigner, he famously remarked that "an army marches on its stomach," offering a prize of 12,000 francs to anyone who could devise a method of preserving food to help keep troops on the move. After fourteen or so years of experiment, it was Nicolas Appert (1749–1841) who won the prize, in January 1810, for his technique of preserving food in sealed bottles.

It is said that one of the first foods he managed to preserve in this way was his version of **chicken supreme** and as a result the dish was exported around Europe at a speed never previously known. His book *L'Art de conserver les substances animales et végétales* ("The Art of Preserving Meat and Vegetables") was published the same year, the first cookbook on modern preservation methods. Within ten years, canning had evolved, based on the technique established by Appert, who was known thereafter as the "father of canning" and his technique as "appertization."

But how did chicken supreme became chicken Kiev? According to the Russian food historian William Pokhlebkin—his surname deriving from *pokhlebka*, or "stew," the underground nickname adopted by his father during the 1917 Revolution—the Russian version of the recipe was invented in the Moscow Merchants' Club in the early twentieth century. This was at a time when Communist Russia rejected everything outside its borders and only Russian names were tolerated. The canny chef at the club renamed the dish chicken Kiev and it became hugely popular as a result. The twentieth century also saw a huge wave of Russian immigrants escaping persecution in their homeland. Many traveled to America and restaurants, particularly on the East Coast, began to call chicken supreme chicken Kiev to attract new customers familiar with the dish from their native land. It was during the two world wars that the new name would have migrated back to Europe. In 1976, chicken Kiev made history by becoming the first ready meal produced and sold by London retailer Marks & Spencer, another step in a different revolution—the conquest of the kitchen by FAST FOOD.

In an ironic footnote to the overall story, despite Nicolas

Appert's success in inventing a process directly leading to the mass production of tin cans, it would be nearly fifty years before another inventor came up with the can opener. Now, that's worth thinking about for a moment.

Possibly the First Curry Ever to Reach New York City

This unusually named curry originated in India, as we would expect, although it very quickly became a staple favorite in the South from the early nineteenth century, thought to have been taken to Georgia by a British sea captain formerly stationed in Bengal, a northeastern region of India. Originally known as Spatchcock chicken, dressed with onions and stewed with curry spices, the name for the dish is thought to have evolved in the United States as a result of the trade between India and the southern ports during the late eighteenth century and mid-nineteenth century, a trade known in India as "country trade." The skippers of the "country ships" involved were universally respected as "country captains," and the mild curry dish was clearly a favorite among them.

The first written reference to **country captain chicken** can be traced to 1857 and a Philadelphia publication called *Miss Leslie's New Cookery Book*, which credits legendary New York restaurant Delmonico's chef Alessandro Filippini as the architect of the dish. But its Southern roots cannot be doubted, and Filippini would have been given the recipe to try, quite possibly the first curry to appear in New York and in that sense something of a novelty. During the 1940s, Franklin D. Roosevelt (1882–1945) and Army General George Patton (1885–1945) dined together on country captain chicken at Warm Springs, Georgia, and their praise for the flavors established the recipe as a state favorite.

The president had made the tiny city of only a few hundred residents his home in 1924 when he built a house there for his visits to the naturally heated springs that relieved his polio-related paraplegia. The only home he ever owned, called Little White House, and where he died, is now a public museum, and his polio hospital is now the Roosevelt Warm Springs Institute for Rehabilitation.

In 2000, the army honored General Patton's favorite recipe by including country captain chicken as one of their packaged MREs (meals ready to eat) to be shipped and prepared for soldiers in the field, and in January 2009, the dish was still popular enough to be a featured recipe in the *New York Times Magazine*.

Bangers and Mash: Exploding Food from the Trenches

No book about the history and origin of food would be complete without the staple English fare of **bangers and mash**. A simple **sausage** and potato dish, it is second only in the hearts and minds of the English people to FISH AND CHIPS (see also HOT DOG). The "mash" part of the name is easy to work out, but where does "bangers" come from?

The sausage, one of the oldest types of processed food in history, can be traced back to ancient times. The Greek philosopher and author Epicharmus (540–450 BC), considered to be the first comedy playwright, wrote a comedy called *Orya* ("The Sausage"), with lots of ribald references to its shape, while the epic poet Homer (c. 850 BC) makes reference to a type of blood sausage in the *Odyssey*. Originally made from entrails stuffed into lengths of animal intestine, sausages are a little more sophisticated these days, unless you are a fan of black pudding or HAGGIS, both harking back to earlier times.

Today, sausages are made from all sorts of meat, including pork, beef, lamb, venison, and chicken, and a vast range of herbs and spices, and sometimes meat is omitted altogether.

British pork sausages, similar to those of France and Italy, began to be mass-produced during the nineteenth century. The Victorians, skeptical of what was actually in a sausage, nicknamed them "Little Bags of Mystery," an expression that seems to have evolved around 1850, based on the suspicion that they were filled with horsemeat. Following the outbreak of World War I in 1914, food shortages and rationing led to a reduction in the amount of meat in a sausage, from whatever animal. Instead, producers packed them out with scraps, cereal, and water, which caused them to pop and hiss when cooked over an open fire on a shovel in the trenches of northern Europe. As a result, the Tommies nicknamed them "bangers" and the phrase "bangers and mash" caught on, already well established by 1919 when soldiers were returning to their old lives.

How Goulash Helped Overthrow Oppression

Ostensibly just another beef stew, **goulash** has more to it than meets the eye, for it turns out to have been both the earliest example of the bouillon cube and an expression of national identity. The dish can be traced back as far as the ninth century, to the cattle ranchers of the proudly independent Magyar tribes living in the Great Plain of Hungary. Before traveling great distances with their flocks, they would slowly casserole diced meat with onions and spices, cooking it until all the liquid was absorbed and then drying it in the sun before storing it away in bags made from the stomach lining of a sheep. This portable food would then be unpacked at night, popped into a pan of water, and boiled up into a soup or stew. In Hungary the dish is called *pörkölt*, and it is still served both as a soup and as a stew, depending on how much water is added: the rest of the world knows it as "goulash," deriving from the Hungarian word *gulyás*, meaning "cowboy" or "cattle herder."

Goulash remained a peasant dish until the end of the eighteenth century and a rise in national awareness throughout the country. As part of the Austro-Hungarian Empire, Hungary was under the rule of the Austrian Hapsburg emperors, who at that time were intent upon homogenizing their territories. Fearing that their national heritage was under threat, Hungarians eagerly embraced anything that expressed their cultural identity. It became imperative to protect the Hungarian tongue (German had become the national language) and every aspect of the traditional Hungarian way of life, including its gastronomy. Hence goulash became highly fashionable, the dish that had until then been eaten only by herdsmen now served in castles and palaces. Like HAGGIS for the Scots, goulash became a symbol of Hungarian identity in the face of oppression. The dish's growing popularity was helped by the introduction of paprika around this time, a smoky spice made from dried red peppers that has become a signature of Hungary and an essential ingredient of goulash as we know it today.

After World War II, Hungary fell again under the control of another oppressive regime, the USSR, and a Stalinist system, political and economic, was imposed upon the country despite growing dissent and protest. In October 1956, a spontaneous revolt took place, starting as a student demonstration and spreading nationwide. The government fell and the revolt continued to spread until the Soviets sent in troops to suppress it. Thousands were arrested, the rebel leader was executed, and a puppet government installed. Ten years of severe repression followed, but by 1966, this had gradually given way to attempts at economic reform. It marked the beginning of what is sometimes called *goulash communism*, deriving from the notion that the stew, like the politics of a country, is made up of a mixture of ingredients. In Hungary, goulash communism represented a discreet attempt by the government to introduce elements of capitalism without acknowledging that there had been any deviation from a socialist economy, in the knowledge that any open dissent from the Soviet system would be brutally put down. This gradually paved the way for independence, which was formally declared in 1989. So you can see how having a national dish can be vital for a country's survival, sustaining its people in both a literal and a symbolic way.

How Does Meat Become Jerky?

Developed by the Quechua tribes of the Andes in South America, *charqui* (literally "dried meat") was a traditional way of curing meat—usually llama, horse, or beef—so that it could be stored for long periods, making it an ideal food for travelers. The technique was picked up by European settlers, who would lay thin strips of beef to dry in the sun, or beside a fire, and then use it on their long journeys across the continent. They called it **jerky** and it remains popular to this day, albeit in a highly processed form. The Quechua word also transferred, via the slave trade, to the Caribbean and to Jamaica in particular, where **jerk** describes a traditional way of grilling meat over a hardwood fire—originally on a framework of sticks (see BARBECUE) and now in a steel drum known as a "jerk pan"—in which meat or fish is rubbed with a special mixture of spices known as **Jamaican jerk spice**.

What Is the Difference Between Shepherd's and Cottage Pie?

Europe's growing enthusiasm for the potato (see "The Rise and Fall of the Potato," page 108) and, crucially, its high yield in a small space meant that by the beginning of the eighteenth century every farmer and peasant was growing their own in whatever bits of land they could find. The combination of "meat and potatoes," with its perfect balance of protein and carbohydrate, soon became the epitome of a square meal for the working man, so much so that it started to be used figuratively, to mean the fundamental part or basis of something. And that meant that, despite their more primitive cooking arrangements, peasants could now make their own version of the pies that had become such a feature of noble banquets. Instead of the inedible huff paste (see "A Brief History of the Pie," page 237), however, every bit of these pragmatic dishes was intended to be eaten, including the topping of cooked potato (either mashed or sliced) that replaced the pastry.

The addition of potato also helped eke out the remains of the SUNDAY ROAST for further meals. And once mincing machines became common in the 1870s, ordinary folk and shepherds alike could shred the meat for their potato pies.

COTTAGE PIE

First mentioned in 1791, **cottage pie** is a simple minced-beef dish bulked out with onions and other vegetables. The cottagers themselves were farm laborers who survived on a basic diet of potatoes and whatever scraps and offcuts they could salvage from previous meals. The name may well have emerged as a joking reference to the roofs of rural cottages: the top layer of potato browned in the oven giving the pie its own thatched roof, as it were. In a similar way, COTTAGE CHEESE was so called because it, too, was made by farm laborers in their homes, using any milk left over after making butter and as a speedy and cheap alternative to hard cheese.

SHEPHERD'S PIE

A later version, made, as the name suggests, with lamb instead of beef, is **shepherd's pie**. Not mentioned until the 1870s, the dish would have evolved in exactly the same way, chiefly in the north of England and in Scotland, where sheep provided the main source of income for highland farmers. Minced lamb and potatoes were cheap and readily available, becoming the staple diet of land workers in these areas.

Both names have since been used almost interchangeably, regardless of whether the principal ingredient is beef or lamb, although many British cooks insist on differentiating between them. In America, cottage pie is now called for obvious reasons **cowboy's pie**. Canada and Australia appear to be less fussy (perhaps due to the decided lack of thatched cottages), happy to go with "shepherd's pie" for both dishes.

10
Indian Cuisine

Exploring for Peppercorns and Discovering Chilies

The Story of Curry

Vindaloo: A Portuguese Dish in Indian Guise

Chutney: Essential Accompaniment
to an Indian Meal

Tale of the Raj: The Invention of
Mulligatawny Soup

"A chilli," said Rebecca, gasping. "Oh, yes!" She thought a chilli was something cool, as its name imported, and was served with some. "How fresh and green they look," she said, and put one into her mouth. It was hotter than the curry; flesh and blood could bear it no longer. She laid down her fork. "Water, for Heaven's sake, water!" she cried.

WILLIAM MAKEPEACE THACKERAY, *Vanity Fair*

Exploring for Peppercorns and Discovering Chilies

In medieval Europe BLACK PEPPER was the king of the spices, essential to cooking and used by the rich and privileged. Pepper was always expensive, but when the Ottomans captured Constantinople in 1453, the easiest trade route to the East was blocked and its price began to spiral out of control, going up by 400 percent between 1496 and 1505 alone. Hence it became imperative to find a new route to the East, in particular India and the Spice Islands. Christopher Columbus (c. 1451–1506) decided to take a different approach: when he set sail in 1492, he was convinced that if he simply kept heading west he would find a new source of pepper and a passage to the East. This was based, of course, on the notion that the world is round, an untested theory at the time. Perceived wisdom of the day insisted the earth was flat, and people waited confidently for news that Columbus had sailed off the edge and into infinity. To many of his sailors, such a fate was, quite literally, just over the horizon.

Landing in the islands of the Caribbean, he was convinced that he had reached the East by going the other way round the globe, especially when he noticed how the inhabitants ate their food very heavily seasoned with hot spices. In particular they used a vegetable they called *ají*. This was the first time a European had come across a **chili pepper**. Columbus was so sure that this was a type of the pepper that he and the backers of his voyage were so keen to find (he had no idea what kind of plant he was looking for, after all) that he named it "pepper of the Indies." Although he had actually discovered both chilies and America, Columbus remained sure until the end of his life that he had succeeded in his original aims. And that's why the chili has been called a pepper ever since. America, on the other hand, wasn't named after its reluctant discoverer but another explorer, Amerigo Vespucci (1454–1512), who was the first to identify the New World of North and South America and realize it wasn't Asia after all.

A few years later, the Portuguese explorer Vasco da Gama (1460/1469–1524) discovered the elusive route to India; the Portuguese (see VINDALOO) promptly seized control of the pepper trade and became the richest nation in the world. They also introduced the chili pepper to India in return, and within thirty years at least three different types were growing along the Malabar Coast (today's Goa and Kerala). The Indians then started exporting the dried spice to Europe in such vast quantities that within a few years it was believed to have originated in India.

The Story of Curry

Britain's oldest cookbook, dating back to the fourteenth century and the kitchens of Richard II, is called *The Forme of Cury*, and its recipes include all kinds of spices from the East, such as nutmeg, cardamom, ginger, and BLACK PEPPER. But two centuries before Vasco da Gama found a safe sea route to India (see CHILI PEPPER), "cury" didn't relate to spices but was merely the Middle English word for cooking. The word we know comes from India and is derived from the Tamil *kari*, meaning a sauce or relish for rice. Its first appearance in print was in a seventeenth-century Portuguese cookbook, which included a recipe for *karil*, a dish very similar to what we would recognize today as **curry**. The fact that the foreign term has been adopted so completely that it has blotted out the memory of the older word is a vivid indication of how important curry has become in Western cuisine.

Legends abound when it comes to explaining how the squeamish Brits developed a taste for this exotic dish. One that tries to grab the word back for the British recounts the tale of a nineteenth-century soldier, Sir George Curry, who served with the East India Company before becoming a general in the Indian army. Curry, we are told, was the first Briton to develop a liking for the highly spiced local food and tried, on several occasions, to introduce it to the English foot soldiers under his command, causing widespread revolt and mutiny. Starved into submission, the men eventually caved in, however, and then found they had developed quite a liking for it.

Yet as *The Forme of Cury* shows, the British have always had a predilection for highly spiced food. And in the days before the tin can (see CHICKEN KIEV), when the only food remaining from home would be weevil-ridden SHIP'S BIS-CUIT, soldiers would have had no choice but to eat locally. Meanwhile, as the influence of the British in India grew, so did the interest in Indian food back in Britain, leading to the publishing of recipes and the commercial creation of curry powder in 1780. In fact the recipe that turned into WORCES-TERSHIRE SAUCE consisted of a curry powder added to vinegar. The first appearance of curry on a menu was in 1773, while the first establishment dedicated to Indian cuisine was the Hindostanee Coffee House at 34 George Street, London, set up in 1809.

Indian cuisine as we know it today is actually a ragbag of different culinary styles—an amalgam of the most appealing aspects of the cuisines of successive waves of invaders and traders to the Indian subcontinent. The Mongolians brought their hotpot cooking, and Chinese traders introduced the stir-frying and the sweet-and-sour sauces that feature in many curries. From the Persians (the Mughals) came rich creamy **korma**, with dried fruit and nuts. The **biryani** (literally "fried food"), consisting of rice and meat layered together, is also a Persian-derived dish. While the **tandoori**— from tandoor, the traditional clay oven used for cooking the food in—came originally from the Middle East. Its name derives from the Babylonian word *tinuru*, meaning "fire"; Hebrew and Arabic then made it *tannur*, evolving into *tandur* in Turkey and Central Asia, and *tandoor* in India and Pakistan.

Europeans trading with India took home many spices, along with lavish fabrics and precious stones, but they exchanged other items in return. Through these traders, potatoes, chilies, and tomatoes were introduced to the subcontinent. Although some Indians were initially suspicious of tomatoes (see also GAZPACHO), seeing them as bloodlike, they were soon adopted into the nation's cuisine. Some aspects of European cooking were also incorporated (see VINDALOO). The British contributed the least of all to Indian cuisine, although they did make KETCHUP, soup (MULLIGATAWNY), and milky TEA (*chai*) very popular throughout the subcontinent. It was the Indian invasion of British cuisine that had the most resounding impact, turning curry into a national dish.

Vindaloo: A Portuguese Dish in Indian Guise

In Britain a **vindaloo** is assumed to be the very hottest curry and often ordered after closing time by the intoxicated as a trial of strength usually sorely regretted the following morning. The recipe for proper vindaloo comes from Goa, on the west coast of India. The correct spelling of its name, *vindalho*, gives away the ingredients of the main dish, once a Portuguese pork casserole (*carne de vinha d'alhos*), seasoned with *alhos* ("garlic") and *vinho* ("wine"), the latter acting as a preservative that allowed the stew to be eaten over several days. The type of meat shows the strength of the Portuguese influence, as the eating of pork is against both the Hindu and Muslim religions.

The earliest Portuguese settlers in Goa became infamous among fellow European visitors for the degree to which they had become assimilated: they observed many of the same customs and wore the same light clothes as the Goans, bathed at least once a day, a habit not practiced by Europeans at the time, married locally, and happily ate the local food. Their enduring gift to their colony was the CHILI PEPPER (seen as a botanical oddity in Portugal), which was soon growing everywhere and was added by the locals in copious amounts to their food and especially to their interpretation of Portuguese pork stew, so much so that the dish soon became almost unrecognizable—as integrated into Goan cuisine as the Portuguese settlers had become integrated into Goa.

To **butter someone up** is to flatter them with the aim of gaining something to your advantage. Some suggest the expression derives from the smooth way butter spreads on bread, to make it more palatable. And it seems a perfectly plausible explanation, until you visit the Hindu temple in Madurai, Tamil Nadu, that is, supposedly the largest temple in the world. Here guides speak of the ancient custom of throwing butterballs of ghee (the clarified butter used as the basis of all Indian cooking) at statues of the gods, a method of seeking favor termed "buttering up the gods." Another custom, Buddhist this time, may also contribute to the origin of the phrase.

During celebrations for the Tibetan New Year, the lamas at all the monasteries create sculptures or "butter flowers" out of colored butter. These are then traditionally displayed on the fifteenth day of the Tibetan lunar year following a religious ceremony the previous evening. The tradition of creating butter sculptures, presented as offerings to statues of the Buddha, can be traced to the Tang Dynasty (AD 618–907) and the belief that such offerings would bring peace and happiness for the full lunar year. This tradition was known as **buttering up the Buddha**. (For more on the Buddha and food, see PORRIDGE.)

Chutney: Essential Accompaniment to an Indian Meal

No Indian meal would be complete without **chutney**, lime and mango being the most popular varieties. Boiled-down fruits preserved with vinegar and sugar and mixed with spices have been popular in India for centuries, and by the beginning of the sixteenth century, as European explorers opened up trade with India (see CHILI PEPPER), these exotic preserves were being imported to northern Europe as luxury goods. The Hindu word for these spicy accompaniments to a main dish is *catni*, pronounced "chat-ni," which serves as the root for the word we use today when asking for something in which to dip our poppadoms.

Tale of the Raj: The Invention
of Mulligatawny Soup

One food that is not a traditional Indian favorite is soup. Although not an authentic Indian dish, **mulligatawny** stands as a vivid reminder of the days the British got their feet under the table in the Indian subcontinent. And it was all due to trade.

Initially dealing in spices, cotton, and opium, the East India Company rapidly became so successful that it had to protect its trade routes and personnel with private militias. It even bought territory in India to give itself a base in the part of the world where it conducted most of its business. At the time, India was made up of many states and kingdoms, and Company employees soon found themselves getting involved in local politics. With uprisings and power struggles all over the land, it was left to them to restore order and protect their business interests. Under the leadership of Robert Clive (1725–74), rebellions were crushed and great battles were won, including those at Calcutta (of Black Hole fame) in February 1757 and at Plessey four months later. As a result, the East India Company came to rule whole swathes of India, exercising military power and assuming administrative functions, to the exclusion, gradually, of its commercial pursuits. Eventually Queen Victoria's government absorbed the Company and India became an official part of the British Empire.

With Britain now controlling much of the country under the banner of the British Raj (deriving from the Hindi word *raj*, meaning "reign"), order was reestablished and law enforced using a new court system. As British expatriates integrated into the Indian way of life, an Anglo-Indian society began to form, with both cultures adapting to each other, absorbing each other's customs. Mulligatawny arose out of this as an ingenious adaptation necessitated by the British requirement for soup as a separate first course, a concept previously unknown in India. Its name a corruption of the Tamil *milagu-tannir* "pepper-water," the spicy meat soup became so popular with the British stationed there that officials in the Madras Presidency were nicknamed "mulls" after it.

11
Italian Cuisine

From Marco Polo to Spaghetti Trees:
The Origins of Pasta

Bolognese: The Sauce or the School of Art?

Carbonara: A Very Revolutionary Pasta Sauce

Pesto: A Sauce Made with Elbow Grease

How Fettuccine Alfredo Became a Star

Pizza: How a Dish from Naples
Conquered the World

The trouble with eating Italian food is that two or three days later you're hungry again.

GEORGE MILLER

From Marco Polo to Spaghetti Trees: The Origins of Pasta

One of the great food myths is that when Marco Polo returned from the court of Kublai Khan in 1295, he brought **pasta** back to Italy with him. But the Italians had been eating it long before that: a list of the possessions of a dead man, Ponzio Bastone, drawn up in 1279, includes "a basket of dried macaroni," indicating that pasta was already a well-established and valued food years before Marco Polo returned from his epic journey to the East. While many cultures have since antiquity eaten some sort of noodle-like food composed of grain, pasta is made from a particular type of wheat—durum wheat semolina, with a high gluten content—which was unknown in China, where noodles were traditionally made using millet or rice. Another distinguishing feature of pasta is its malleability, which has resulted in the extraordinary range of shapes and sizes that characterize this food.

The truth is that it's difficult to pinpoint when and where pasta was invented. For a start, the name—meaning "dough" and akin to our word "paste"—has only been in common use since the end of World War II. Before that, it would have been known by the names of individual types of pasta rather than this generic term, but they all were forms of the same thing. And it goes back a long way. Alan Davidson, in *The Penguin Companion to Food* (2002), describes an Etruscan relief from 400 BC that shows a set of perfect pasta-making tools. The Romans had their own kind of pasta dish (see LASAGNA for more on this), and a text of 1154 describes people in Palermo, Sicily—where durum wheat, the basic ingredient of modern pasta, had been introduced by the Arabs in the seventh century—making strings of dough that they were already exporting all round the world. By 1351, Boccaccio was writing in the *Decameron* of a fantastical mythical land whose inhabitants rolled macaroni down mountains made of grated cheese. And by the sixteenth century, thanks to Catherine de Médicis and her introduction of Italian cooking to France (see EGGS FLORENTINE and "From Fine Sauces to Haute Cuisine," page 139), pasta began to catch on throughout Europe.

Pasta has been integral to Italy's national identity ever since. When Mussolini's enemies rumored that he was planning to ban the consumption of pasta because he felt it was responsible for the low state of the Italian people, there were riots and protests. (The reverse was true, in fact: Mussolini regarded it as so important that he wanted to dedicate more land to growing wheat and turn Italy into a self-sufficient producer.) The only outspoken critics of pasta were the Futurists, the artistic movement of the early twentieth century that despised tradition of any kind, including Italy's national dish, which it denounced as "a symbol of oppressive dullness, plodding deliberation and fat-bellied conceit." Somewhat unsurprisingly, the movement didn't last long—its supporters would have been too hungry to keep it going.

There are more than six hundred different types of pasta, in every conceivable shape and with exotic names to match. Here's a little more on the six most interesting varieties:

SPAGHETTI

Spaghetti (see also SPAGHETTI BOLOGNESE) is thought to account for over two-thirds of the annual pasta consumption around the world, although it only became popular during the late nineteenth century when the introduction of factories with powerful extrusion presses meant that it could be mass-produced. Prior to this, it would have been made by hand, a time-consuming and complicated process. The word *spaghetti* translates as "thin strings." Hence when Galileo Galilei (1564–1642) wrote that he had "attached two balls to spaghetti" for one of his experiments, this didn't necessarily mean he had been playing with his food. The Italians only started associating the word with thin strips of pasta in the early nineteenth century; its first recorded use is from 1836, and it would be another fifty years before it became common parlance elsewhere in Europe. Since then, spaghetti's profile has risen so high that it is regarded as the defining type of pasta and, aside from PIZZA, the food most associated with Italy. So much so that, during the 1960s, Americans even began calling their low-budget cowboy films—produced and directed by Italians and shot in Spain or Italy—**spaghetti westerns**.

VERMICELLI

Vermicelli, essentially extra-fine spaghetti, is most notable for the meaning of its name: "little worms." An even thinner type is called **capelli d'angelo**, which translates as "angel's hair." A recipe for vermicelli first appeared in a very specialized cookbook, *De arte coquinaria per vermicelli e maccaroni siciliani* ("The Art of Cooking Sicilian Vermicelli and Macaroni"), written in the fifteenth century by Martino da Como, highly respected for his culinary knowledge and possibly the world's first "celebrity" chef.

RAVIOLI AND TORTELLINI

Consisting of a filling between two thin layers of pasta, **ravioli** were first mentioned in the fourteenth century, in the writings of Francesco di Marco, a merchant of Prato, and in *The Forme of Cury* (see CURRY), where they appear as "rauioles." But the type of stuffed pasta that has most caught the Italian imagination is **tortellini** (from *tortello*, "small cake"). Originating from the Italian towns of Bologna and Modena, the food has a number of legends explaining how it was invented. According to one of these, Lucrezia Borgia (1480–1519), the FLORENTINE beauty and infamous poisoner, was staying at a small inn in Modena. The innkeeper was so captivated by her that he couldn't resist the urge to peek into her room through the keyhole, to try and see her naked. But from his vantage point and in the dim candlelight, he could only make out her navel. Even so, according to the story, this was enough to send him into an ecstasy that inspired him to create tortellini—with its distinctive umbilical shape—that very evening. A more widely accepted explanation is that tortellini is based on the shape of a turtle, in an attempt to replicate the famous symbol of Modena, many of whose buildings bear the turtle motif.

MACARONI

Macaroni, a tubular form of pasta, was probably one of the first pastas to be made. While its name is believed by some etymologists to derive from the Italian *ammaccare*, meaning "to crush," the *Oxford English Dictionary* suggests that it comes from the Greek *makaria*, "food made from barley," which is also the root of "macaroon" (although, as its chief ingredient is ground almonds, that might seem to point to the first derivation). Macaroni was so popular in former times that its name was used as a generic term for pasta. In

England during the eighteenth century, the word was also used as a pejorative term for a metrosexual—typically, fashionable young men who had been to Italy on the Grand Tour and returned full of continental affectation in their speech and dress. The item most associated with the *macaroni* was an immensely tall white wig whose powdered curls might be thought to resemble tubular pasta.

LASAGNA

The oldest pasta of all is **lasagna**. It's suggested that the word may derive from the Roman *lasanum*, meaning a cooking pot, a term that was subsequently applied to the dish. Or that it might come from the Greek *laganon* (*lagana* in the plural), a flat sheet of pasta cut into strips. Indeed, Horace, writing in the first century BC, talks of *lagana*, fine sheets of dough that were fried and consumed as an everyday food. Likewise, an early cookbook, from the fifth century, describes a dish called *lagana* that consisted of layers of dough with meat stuffing and that could perhaps be the ancestor of the modern dish. It certainly seems to have been established by the thirteenth century: Marco Polo, in his writings on the Orient, mentions eating a "lasagna" made using flour from the breadfruit, implying that he was already familiar with the more conventional version of the dish, made from wheat flour.

The first cookbook to appear in print—Platina's *De honesta voluptate et valetudine* ("On honorable pleasure and health"), published in 1474—gives the instruction that a certain type of PASTA should be cooked for the amount of time it takes to say the Lord's prayer three times. That is a remarkably short time even for fresh pasta and shows how, even then, the Italians preferred their pasta chewy or **al dente**. In Italian this means "to the tooth" or "to the bite," indicating that the cook should pop a piece of the pasta in their mouth and, if it still offers some resistance when bitten, then it is cooked to perfection. Leave it in the pan much longer and it will become overly soft and lose its texture. Leave it in for too short a time and it will stick to the teeth when chewed; not so much "to the tooth" as "on the tooth" and definitely undercooked.

Bolognese: The Sauce or the School of Art?

Ask anybody in the little town of Bologna about **spaghetti bolognese** and they will insist there is no such thing. Ironically enough, they much prefer tagliatelli or LASAGNA. However, to the rest of the pasta-loving world, the "sauce from Bologna" (bolognese)—typically made with minced beef and chopped vegetables in a tomato sauce (although authentic recipes use stock and wine and no tomato)—is famously mixed with SPAGHETTI and sprinkled with PARMESAN CHEESE. In Bologna, they call the sauce *ragù alla bolognese*, *ragù* coming from the French word *ragoût*, meaning "stew."

The people of Bologna themselves are far prouder of the

Bolognese Artists, a group of painters who emerged from the Bologna School of Painting and who so dominated the cultural scene from 1582 until 1700 that Bologna rivaled Rome and Florence as the center of the Italian arts. Consisting of Annibale Carracci, his brother Agostino, and their cousin Ludovico, the Carracci, as they were collectively known, led the group of painters into what became known as the great century of Bolognese painting. The talent the Carracci fostered around the world through their tuition has secured their place in history, although I imagine most people will be more familiar with the town's spaghetti sauce than they are with its painters.

Carbonara: A Very Revolutionary Pasta Sauce

Second only to SPAGHETTI BOLOGNESE, **spaghetti carbonara**— the sauce made with BACON, eggs, garlic, and BLACK PEPPER— must be one of the most popular pasta dishes of them all. The name *carbonara* derives from the Italian word for "charcoal," which has led to the theory that the dish was first devised as a hearty meal for the charcoal burners working in the forests around Rome. An alternative suggestion is that the copious amounts of black pepper added to the dish look like flakes of charcoal, and hence the name.

There is a more interesting theory, however, one that also revolves around the connection with charcoal. The Carbonari (literally "charcoal men") were a group of freedom fighters who formed a secret society in Naples around 1808 with the sole intention of overthrowing the foreign government imposed by Napoleon in 1805, when the upstart Frenchman declared himself King of Italy. Using coded language based on the occupation of charcoal burning, they would meet in forest huts that they called "places of selling charcoal," while many of their rituals were drawn from the Freemasons of Italy and France. After Napoleon's final defeat at Waterloo in 1815, Austria once again became the dominant power in Italy, successfully crushing uprisings by leading members of the Carbonari, notably in 1821 and 1831.

Carbonari members Giuseppe Mazzini (1805–72) and Garibaldi fought both political and military campaigns throughout their lives and are remembered as the leading figures of the Italian Risorgimento (resurgence), a movement intent upon Italian unification. It was Mazzini who, in 1831, believing the Carbonaris' influence to be waning, formed a new secret society, La Giovine Italia (Young Italy), which rose to become the most significant revolutionary group in Europe, paving the way for the unification of Italy in 1861.

There is, however, no record of the Carbonaris' preferred sauce for pasta, or whether it was made using bacon and eggs. Indeed, there is no record of the dish until after World War II, when it was taken back to America by troops stationed in Italy, leading to *spaghetti alla carbonara* becoming hugely popular. Some say that it was the soldiers themselves who invented the dish, handing over their ration of bacon and eggs to local Italian chefs, who transformed the ingredients into the famous sauce.

Pesto: A Sauce Made with Elbow Grease

Originating in Genoa and typically consisting of a mixture of basil, garlic, pine nuts, grated cheese, and olive oil, **pesto** is most commonly served with pasta. The derivation of the word, from the Italian *pestare*, "to crush" or "to pound," reveals how the dish is prepared: by grinding the ingredients together, traditionally using a pestle and mortar. Interestingly, "pestle" has a similar root, from the Old French *pestel*, taken in turn from the Latin *pistillum*, which derives from *pinsere*, "to pound." It shares this derivation with **pistou**, the Provençal version of pesto, made in the same way and using all the same ingredients except pine nuts. The earliest reference to a dish resembling pesto (or pistou) can be found in Roman textbooks and a cheese spread called *moretum*, to which basil would have been added following the Roman conquest of north Africa, where the herb is believed to have originated. Now, of course, no Italian dish would be complete without a scattering of fresh basil leaves.

How Fettuccine Alfredo Became a Star

This dish, of **fettuccine** tossed with PARMESAN CHEESE and butter, is said to have been created in 1914 by Alfredo di Lelio at his restaurant, Alfredo alla Scrofa, in Rome. He made it for his pregnant wife who was suffering badly from morning sickness and finding it difficult to keep most things down. American chefs also add shrimp, garlic, and green vegetables (high in folic acid, incidentally), such as broccoli or parsley. **Fettuccine Alfredo** soon became the restaurant's signature dish and popular with American tourists after World War I.

Di Lelio's restaurant became world famous in 1927 when Douglas Fairbanks, the most recognized film star on the planet at the time, booked a table while on honeymoon with Mary Pickford. The restaurateur made such a performance of serving his fettuccini Alfredo to the couple that they fell in love with it. To show their appreciation, Fairbanks returned the following day with a golden spoon and fork, which he presented to the restaurant, along with a framed photograph of themselves that di Lelio proudly hung on the wall. On returning to America, Fairbanks and Pickford served the dish whenever they held a dinner party, and news of the recipe soon spread between the chefs of Hollywood and beyond.

Pizza: How a Dish from Naples Conquered the World

Pizza, the signature Italian dish that is a favorite in just about every country in the world, wasn't actually invented in Italy. The ancestor of the modern dish was created thousands of years ago by the ancient Greeks and Persians. It is said that soldiers of the Persian king Darius I (521–486 BC) baked a type of flatbread—in an improvised oven made by placing their shields over their camp fires—which they covered with cheese and dates. The ancient Greeks, meanwhile, served a similar type of bread, which they covered with cheese, herbs, and olive oil. Indeed, it is thought that there could be an etymological connection between the Greek **pita** and the Italian "pizza," which is believed to have evolved from the Old German *pizzo*, meaning "to bite." The first recorded use of the word was in AD 997 in a Latin text from Gaeta, a southern Italian port near Naples, which has remained the home of the pizza ever since.

Pizza was a cheap and filling way to eke out the contents of a bare pantry, and the people of Naples were famously poverty-stricken. In 1830, the French writer and food expert Alexandre Dumas, père (1802–70), wrote how the Neapolitan poor subsisted on pizza during the winter and that it was typically flavored with "oil, lard, tallow, cheese, tomato, or anchovies."

It was the arrival of thousands of Italian immigrants in America in the last two decades of the nineteenth century that introduced the rest of the world to pizza. At first it was served as a street food, as it had been in Italy, but once the first pizzeria opened in Little Italy in New York City, in 1905, pizza spread like wildfire. The first pizza vendors sold versions of the dish they had eaten in their home country, but soon all kinds of variations slipped in. A favorite topping was pepperoni, which became so popular that a cheese and pepperoni pizza is now known throughout the world as an **American**. Today, pizzas are topped with a wide range of other ingredients, although the Neapolitan style still predominates. Here are three modern varieties:

MARINARA

Topped with tomato, oregano, garlic, and olive oil, **marinara** is the oldest and most basic type of Neapolitan pizza. The full name—*pizza alla marinara*, or "sailor-style pizza"—reflects its seafaring origins. This was a dish that might well have been prepared by *la marinara*, the sailor's wife, for her husband, either to sustain him on a sea voyage or to feed him on his return. These days some chefs interpret the name to mean a sauce or topping containing seafood, but that does not reflect the original, authentic version of the dish.

MARGHERITA

Another type of Neapolitan pizza, made with a topping of tomato, mozzarella, basil, and olive oil, links an Italian queen with the country's poorest city. Margherita Maria Theresa Giovanna of Savoy, born in Turin on November 20, 1851, was the daughter of Ferdinand, Duke of Genoa, and his wife, Elizabeth of Saxony. With such a privileged background, it is hardly surprising that Margherita's future was planned long in advance, and on April 21, 1868, aged just sixteen, she was married to Umberto, the heir to the Italian throne. Margherita became queen in 1878 when Umberto succeeded as the second King of Italy, now a unified country (see CARBONARA), and her passionate patronage of the arts and outspoken support for organizations such as the Red Cross earned her the respect of the young nation.

Indeed, she was held in such affection that the third highest mountain in Africa was named after her, Margherita Peak (which you could translate as "Mount Daisy," as that is the meaning of her name in Italian), and she is also commemorated in a culinary way. It was a visit by the popular queen to Naples in 1889 that prompted Raffaelle Esposito, owner of the Pizzaria di Pietro, to prepare a special meal in her honor. Using the colors of the new national flag, green, white, and red, Esposito combined cheese and tomato with basil to create what has become one of the world's biggest-selling pizzas, and the base ingredients for most of the others. He called it **pizza Margherita** (daisy pizza, in other words, although that doesn't sound quite as appetizing) after his queen. And so it's been called ever since.

CALZONE

The pizza equivalent of a PASTY or a savory turnover, the **calzone** has all the normal filling of a pizza but is folded in half, which makes it much easier to eat on the move. In reference to its less-than-glamorous looks, *calzone* means "trouser leg" or "drooping sack." It is typically served with marinara sauce for dipping.

It is estimated that U.S. citizens eat an average twenty-three pounds of pizza, per person, per year. And that makes the pizza second only to the HAMBURGER as their favorite food.

12
Chinese Cuisine

Chinese Food for Thought

Dim Sum: Afternoon Tea Chinese-Style

When Spring Rolls into Summer

Peking Duck: A Very Rich Snack

The Less Than All-American Story of Chop Suey

I find chopsticks frankly distressing. Am I alone in thinking it odd that a people ingenious enough to invent paper, gunpowder, kites, and any number of other useful objects, and who have a noble history extending back three thousand years, haven't yet worked out that a pair of knitting needles is no way to capture food?

BILL BRYSON

Chinese Food for Thought

To Western eyes, Chinese cuisine is hugely varied and complex, its delicacies ranging from a soup made out of bird's nests to sweet-and-sour pork. One way of understanding how it all works is to explore how the two major philosophies that have indelibly influenced Chinese culture—Taoism and Confucianism—have affected the way Chinese people cook and enjoy their food.

TAOISM

Taoism is based on the teachings of Lao Tse, who lived around the sixth century BC and was said to have been a teacher of Confucius. It revolves around the concept of the Tao, the guiding force behind the universe that holds everything in balance and that incorporates the principles of yin and yang, opposing yet complementary forces that are present in everything, including food. Taoists believe that either yin or yang predominates in a particular food, "yin" foods having cooling properties and "yang" foods warming ones. For a dish to be properly balanced, therefore, it is important to get the right mixture of yin and yang elements. Cooking methods come into the equation, too, boiling and steaming being regarded as yin techniques and frying and roasting as yang.

Based on these concepts, meals should be carefully prepared and balanced and gluttony and snacking avoided (for more on this, see the origins of DIM SUM). As well as being better for the health, the idea of not eating too much may hark back to a belief in a golden age where people didn't need to eat at all but simply got by on the cosmic "qi" or energy of yin and yang. Raw food shouldn't be consumed to excess either, as Taoists believe that it creates internal weakness from too much cold energy in the stomach. For this reason, all vegetables have to be prepared in various ways, steamed or stir-fried at the very least. The health benefits of a dish are important, too, food being regarded as preventative of disease, and every ingredient in a dish should contribute to its overall healthiness. Ginger is a particular Taoist favorite, for instance, taken both as a digestive aid and to help reduce high blood pressure. With so much to keep in mind, the Taoist chef must be reaching for the ginger at every opportunity.

CONFUCIANISM

Confucius (551–479 BC) was a philosopher whose teachings still remain crucial to the Chinese state of mind. Born into a period of anarchy and constant war, all his teachings were focused on establishing a sense of balance and order in the world. He believed in the importance of education and self-improvement and that people should cultivate themselves morally so that they refrained from doing wrong, living in harmony with each other. And he attached great importance to food, which he saw as one of the three essential requirements for a successful society (the other two being an army and mutual trust). Confucius stressed that for a meal to be both nutritious and a pleasant experience, each dish should have the right blend of color, flavor, aroma, and texture—something that remains central to Chinese cuisine today. As in Taoism, ingredients should be balanced: the fatty richness of PEKING DUCK, for instance, offset by a salad of spring onions, and sweet flavors counterbalanced by sour. It was he who taught the Chinese that it was barbaric (and dangerous) to bring knives to the dining table. And ever since then, Chinese food has been served in bite-size pieces and eaten with chopsticks. Another food-related principle that the great thinker adhered to was never to eat alone: meals should be a shared activity, with people enjoying each other's company as well as the food. Interestingly, he also taught that an excellent cook must first become an excellent matchmaker.

Dim Sum: Afternoon Tea Chinese-Style

The culinary art of **dim sum** began centuries ago, as a form of refreshment for the merchants and traders along the Silk Road, the route connecting China's lucrative silk trade with the Middle East, Africa, and Europe. Teahouses cropped up along the way to provide travelers with a place to rest. At first, it was considered inappropriate to combine TEA with food, because it was believed it might lead to excessive weight gain, which was against Taoist teachings (see "Chinese Food for Thought," page 215). But when it was later decided that tea aided digestion, teahouse owners began adding various light snacks, which became hugely popular and evolved into the tradition of dim sum.

Literally translated as "touching the heart," because it is only meant to be a snack not a main meal, dim sum typically consists of small steamed items, such as dumplings of pork or shrimp, SPRING ROLLS, meatballs, or rice wrapped in lotus leaves, all served in bamboo steamer baskets. This form of Cantonese TAPAS is served in restaurants at any time of day between sunrise and the main evening meal and is always taken with tea. In fact, the Chinese invitation to go and partake of dim sum is "let's go and **yum cha**," which actually means "let's drink tea," so closely are the two activities related. One, it seems, always goes with the other. (In Australia, yum cha has even become the preferred term for dim sum.)

When partaking in dim sum, it is customary to pour tea for your fellow diners before filling your own cup. They will then thank you by tapping their bent index and middle fingers together on the table. The Chinese have a legend about the origin of this gesture, according to which an emperor went in disguise to drink tea with a friend outside the palace. While at yum cha, the emperor poured his companion some tea, which was deemed a great honor. The companion, not wanting to give away the emperor's identity in public by bowing, instead tapped his index and middle fingers on the table as a coded sign of his appreciation.

Dim sum became more widespread during the Song Dynasty (AD 960–1280), when teahouses flourished all over China. By the time Marco Polo arrived in 1271, teahouses and dim sum were an established part of the Chinese culture, and when the great explorer finally returned to Europe in 1295, he introduced some Chinese artifacts (see PASTA) and traditions, and wrote about many more, but dim sum wasn't among them. Indeed, it wasn't discovered by Westerners until relatively recently, via Chinese immigration to the West. From around the nineteenth century, Chinese communities began appearing in every major city around the world, and "Chinatown" became the place where most immigrants settled. It would have been on a visit to their local Chinatown that Westerners encountered the delights of dim sum for the first time.

These days, the range of dim sum dishes is vast and includes sweet as well as savory items. As it is a style of food, not a particular dish, chefs can be as imaginative as they please and use any manner of frying, boiling, or steaming to create the dishes. The essence of dim sum remains the same, however: everything is served in small portions. Dishes are prepared fresh each day and wheeled around on carts, enabling customers to select whatever they like the look of each time it passes by. Their bill is then calculated as they leave by the number, size, and color of the plates they hand back. It is a system that can be open to abuse (less scrupulous customers hiding or stealing the plates after finishing with them), so servers often keep a tally of the dishes consumed.

When Spring Rolls into Summer

Spring rolls consist of a mixture of meat, seafood, or vegetables wrapped in a layer of thin, unleavened dough and deep-fried. They were originally served as special snacks with TEA (see DIM SUM) when relatives and friends came to visit. Because of its rich golden color when fried, a spring roll is likened to a gold nugget and thus associated with prosperity and good fortune. The English name, which dates back only to 1943, comes from the tradition of serving them on the first day of the Chinese New Year, which is also the first day of spring in the lunar year. But if you order spring rolls in a Vietnamese restaurant, you'll get the healthier raw version—anathema to the Chinese (see "Chinese Food for Thought," page 215)—made with rice paper, shrimp, and fresh herbs, and also known as **summer rolls**.

Peking Duck: A Very Rich Snack

One of the world's great delicacies, roast duck has been a favorite dish in China since antiquity, but **Peking duck** as we'd recognize it today came about somewhat later—during the latter part of the Ming Dynasty (1368–1644), after China had changed its capital from Nanjing to Peking (now Beijing) in 1421. Previously the birds that had been roasted were the small ducks living in the canals around Nanjing, but the relocation of the capital had an unexpected side effect. Feeding on the grains that fell overboard from barges traveling between Nanjing and Peking, the ducks gradually became larger, evolving over the years into a new variety of larger, plumper birds that were then domesticated by Chinese farmers. This meat had so much more fat in it that when roasted, the dish was transformed into a marvel of savory crunchiness. The Chinese then started force-feeding the duck in order to increase its fattiness further (see also FOIE GRAS).

Peking duck, as traditionally eaten by the wealthiest Chinese, consists of just the crisp salted skin, caramelized into a beautiful glossy brown in a long process that takes a whole day. To the Chinese, the dish is all about the taste, the texture, and the expense, not the nutritional value. The meat of the duck was simply used as the means to cook and flavor the skin and was then, like the pastry of a medieval pie (see "A Brief History of the Pie," page 237), given to the servants to eat. Once exported to the West in the twentieth century, the many fans of the dish (known as *canard laqué* in French, literally "varnished duck") misunderstood the preferred Chinese approach and relished both the skin and meat of the duck and traditionally serve it with pancakes, spring onions, and hoisin sauce.

The Less Than All-American Story of Chop Suey

Traditionally seen as an American parody of Chinese food, **chop suey** is surrounded by all kinds of stories about how it was first invented. They all feature a harried immigrant cook forced against his wishes to cook a meal—depending on the version of the story, either by drunken gold miners, angry railway builders, or a visiting Chinese dignitary—at an hour when only scraps were left in his kitchen. He stir-fried these all together into a kind of hash and, when asked by his satisfied customers what the dish was called, announced it was *chop suey*, which was his joke, as it is Cantonese for "odds and ends." (In Mandarin, the name of the dish means cooked animal entrails, which, assuming the cook had them on hand, may not have pleased his American customers quite so much.)

It turns out, however, that chop suey was actually an authentic dish from Toisan, a rural district south of Canton, home of most of the earliest Chinese immigrants to California. The name is *tsap seui* (which does indeed mean "miscellaneous scraps") and it is made up of leftover vegetables and bits of meat stir-fried together. After all, as the most pressing reason for immigration to America was severe poverty, it's not unlikely that the earliest Chinese settlers in Gold Rush California would have been accustomed to reusing and eating scraps and leftovers (see also BUBBLE AND SQUEAK).

13
Christmas Dinner

Who Invented Christmas Dinner?

Why Do We Have a Christmas Ham?

Should It Be Goose or Turkey for Dinner?

Where on a Turkey Is the Parson's Nose?

Celebrating Twelfth Night with
King Cake and Hot Punch

Christmas at my house is always at least six or seven times more pleasant than anywhere else. We start drinking early. And while everyone else is seeing only one Santa Claus, we'll be seeing six or seven.

W. C. FIELDS

Who Invented Christmas Dinner?

When talking about feasting, what better subject to be tackling than the traditional **Christmas dinner**. It is the second most important (and calorific) meal of the year for many of us, but why is it that we feel obligated to gather relatives around that we don't like very much and spend the day feeding them—if only in the hope they explode?

Part of the reason may lie in the fact that it belongs to a tradition of sociable merrymaking that goes back a very long way. Midwinter feasts are a feature of all cultures and religions: generally held on or around the shortest day of the year (December 21), they celebrate the fact that spring isn't far off, with its promise of new life. In Neolithic and Bronze Age times, the winter solstice was immensely important because communities could not be certain that they would actually survive the winter. The feast was an offering to the gods to ensure that they would survive the starvation common in the months between January and April. Tribes slaughtered most of their older cattle so they would not have to be fed during this period, hence it was almost the only time of year when fresh meat was available. The celebrations also had a valuable psychological purpose, cheering people up at the darkest point of the year. Even when life became easier and more civilized, the feasts still continued.

The Romans had celebrated the festival of Sol Invictus (the Unconquered Sun) on December 25, and when the Christian Church came to formalizing its feast days, it pragmatically picked that day as Jesus's birthday, which, of course, it wasn't—the actual date isn't known. As Syrus the Scriptor commented in the late fourth century:

> It was a custom of the pagans to celebrate on the same December 25 the birthday of the Sun, at which they kindled lights in token of festivity. In these solemnities and revelries the Christians also took part. Accordingly, when the doctors of the Church perceived that the Christians had a leaning to this festival, they took council and resolved that the true Nativity should be solemnized on that day.

Traces of these fire festivals can be found in aspects of the Christmas tradition that survive to this day: the Yule log that was kept burning for the twelve days of the festival, still commemorated in the log-shaped French Christmas cake known as the **bûche de Noël**; the candles Victorians fastened to their Christmas trees, today represented by much safer bulbs.

The first recorded Christmas feast took place at Rome in AD 336, and a few years later, in 350, Pope Julius I formally adopted the date as the time to celebrate the birth of Christ. Festivities continued from December 25 until January 6 and the Epiphany (see also TWELFTH NIGHT), marking the visit of the Magi or Three Wise Men to the infant Jesus. Basically, it was a two-week party, a tradition that has remained part of the Christian way of life ever since.

Legend has it that it was on Christmas Day that King Arthur drew Excalibur from the stone, thus proving that he was the rightful king of England, and Arthurian Christmas feasts swell the pages of medieval literature. The fourteenth-century poem *Sir Gawain and the Green Knight* begins in the midst of Christmas revelry at Camelot, where King Arthur, the Knights of the Round Table, and their ladies celebrate "for fully fifteen days, with all the feasting and merrymaking they could think of; such sounds of mirth and merriment, glorious to hear, a pleasant uproar by day, dancing at night." The lavishness of medieval feasts is legendary. As one historian noted in 1398: "[King Richard II] kept his Christmas at Lichfield, where he spent [used] in the Christmastime 200 tunns of wine, and 2,000 oxen with their appurtenances."

These celebrations, with their thinly veiled paganism, have had their detractors, however. In 1583, the Scottish Presbyterians decided that there was no biblical foundation for a Christmas feast day. Christmas only became an official holiday in Scotland once again in 1958. In 1644, Oliver Cromwell's Puritan Parliament banned its celebration—even the word "Christmas" was abolished, with its overtones of the Catholic Mass. Cromwell wanted December 25 to be a purely religious anniversary in which people contemplated the birth of Jesus rather than ate and drank too much. In London, soldiers were ordered to patrol the streets and take, by force if necessary, food being cooked for a Christmas celebration. Traditional Christmas decorations and festive dishes were also banned. However, with the return of Charles II, the Act of Uniformity (1662) overturned the ban, enshrining in law the ceremonies and rites of the Book of Common Prayer, and as the Church of England began to reestablish its authority, Christmas was once again celebrated with all its previous revelry.

The Puritans, who had already been leaving England in droves for over fifty years to set up a more godly new world, weren't entirely averse to a celebration, however. In 1621, to thank God for the success of their very first harvest, the pilgrims of Plymouth Colony held a festival known as the "First Thanksgiving." Celebrated on December 13, Thanksgiving took over from Christmas as the midwinter festival of the new settlers. Then, in 1863, Abraham Lincoln moved Thanksgiving to the end of November, leaving a sufficient breathing

space before Christmas, which now could be properly celebrated once again.

Why Do We Have a Christmas Ham?

In the same way that the Norse word for their pagan midwinter festival—Yule—is used almost synonymously with Christmas, the inclusion of a ham alongside TURKEY for the CHRISTMAS
DINNER shows how the Christian festival has absorbed elements of other midwinter feasts. It was a Norse tradition to
eat wild boar at Yule as a tribute to Freyr, the god of farming,
weather, and fertility, while the Romans ate boar during their
midwinter festival, Saturnalia, held in honor of their god of
agriculture, Saturn. A wild boar is associated with another
figure in classical mythology, Adonis, who died after being
gored by one and who shares certain characteristics with the
story of Jesus, in that a cult of rebirth was associated with
him (after his death he was reborn in the form of a flower, the
anemone) and his birthday was celebrated on the same day,
December 25.

The **Christmas ham** is also linked with the Boar's Head
Feast, which still takes place, although much more rarely
than it used to, and is connected with the ancient tradition of
serving a boar's head at a banquet, where it would have been
the central dish. The wild boar is a ferocious beast and to
have its head on a platter meant that you had vanquished a
formidable enemy. In Christian symbolism, the boar's head
came to represent the triumph of the Christ Child over sin.
The tradition of sacrificing a boar and presenting its head at
a Yuletide feast is described in the oldest Christmas carol in
English, "The Boar's Head Carol" (first printed in 1521),
which is sung at the feast as the boar's head is carried in on a
platter. The current festival originated at Queen's College,

Oxford, where it is still observed every Christmas. The college has its own story, recounted in 1868 by William Henry Husk, who recorded how the tradition arose in

> commemoration of an act of valour performed by a student of the college, who, while walking in the neighbouring forest of Shotover and reading Aristotle, was suddenly attacked by a wild boar. The furious beast came open-mouthed upon the youth, who, however, very courageously, and with a happy presence of mind, thrust the volume he was reading down the boar's throat, crying, *Græcum est* [with the compliments of the Greeks], and fairly choked the savage with the sage.

Should It Be Goose or Turkey for Dinner?

The traditional main dish at Christmas was once **goose**. That was because, like other migratory fowl, geese appeared and disappeared at crucial times in the yearly cycle, so eating them accompanied ceremonial events in the solar and agricultural year. People have linked geese to the changing seasons since antiquity, when different cultures around the world would sacrifice the goose to the gods in thanks for the harvest, then feast on its flesh afterward. Goose was served at the Celtic Samhain, or Halloween, the Norse Yule (see CHRISTMAS HAM), and the Christian Michaelmas. In the Middle Ages there was even a festival known as Wayzgoose, a traditional printers' fête, held at around Michaelmas (the autumn equinox) to mark the end of summer and the beginning of working by candlelight. The master printer would hold a feast for his apprentices and journeymen, with roast goose as the main dish.

The shift from goose to **turkey** at Christmas was due to Thanksgiving celebrations (see CHRISTMAS DINNER) in America. Turkeys are native to northern America, where they live in flocks, roost in swamps, and feed on wild berries and seeds. They are awkward in flight and easy to catch (see page 232 and PARSON'S NOSE), and that made them a perfect food source for early settlers. The colonists initially confused the birds with guineafowl, which were exported from northern India and other parts of Asia via Turkey to Europe and consequently known as "Turkey hens" or "Turkey cocks." Hence the American bird became known as a turkey, a term that, ironically, stuck to this species rather than the one actually imported via the country of the same name.

American settlers served turkey at Thanksgiving, making it the seasonal dish. And in much of the Western world today, turkeys have replaced geese at the Christmas feast. But interestingly, these two birds share the same symbolism. Just as the people of the Old World associated geese with the solar year, so the Native Americans connected turkeys with the sun. According to a Hopi creation myth, it was a male turkey that first tried to raise the sun in the sky, burning his head in the process. And that, apparently, is why turkeys are completely bald.

To **talk turkey** means to have a full and frank discussion. European settlers in America developed a taste for the local delicacy, and soon the gobbler was in high demand. As a result, all serious discussions with the Native Americans became known as "talking about turkey," and the phrase passed into common usage, eventually crossing the water back to Britain. An alternative suggestion for the origin of the phrase comes from turkey hunting. Hunters would attract their prey by making gobbling noises, in imitation of the bird. Apparently the daft creatures would then return the call and so reveal their whereabouts to the hunter.

Going **cold turkey**, by contrast, is considered to be the best way to wean a person off an addiction to something, generally hard drugs. The expression was first recorded in the 1930s, from the observation that the skin of a person withdrawing from drugs is pale and clammy and covered in goose bumps—like the skin of a plucked turkey. Beat writer William Burroughs goes a step further, suggesting in his book *Junkie* (1953) that human skin, during the period of withdrawal, resembles that of a turkey that has not only been plucked, but also cooked and left to cool. That is one explanation, but not all etymologists agree, some believing that the expression goes back further, to 1910, and a comparison between a meal of cold turkey, which requires minimal preparation, and withdrawing from heavy drug use without preparation.

Where on a Turkey Is the Parson's Nose?

The fleshy protuberance at the end of a dressed TURKEY is known anatomically as the pygostyle (from the ancient Greek "rump pillar") and covers the part of a bird's spine to which the tail feathers are attached. Millions of years ago, this is what gave the ancestors of modern birds an advantage over those with completely mobile tails, as the rigid structure was much better for flight control. (Not that turkeys are exactly noted for their flying ability; it's why they made such easy prey for the European settlers in America.) In addition to the turkey, the pygostyle can be found on chicken, GOOSE, and duck alike, and is considered a delicacy by some when roasted until crisp. The French refer to the meat near it as *sot-l'y-laisse*, meaning "only a fool would leave it." Its swollen appearance is thanks to the oil glands a bird uses when cleaning itself, and has led to its common name, **parson's nose**—or the **pope's nose** or **sultan's nose**, depending on who you feel like insulting—based on the notion that it looks like a snooty parson with "his nose in the air." The expression dates back to the Middle Ages at least, as indicated by a carving that appears on the misericord (underside) of a seat in the choir stalls at St. Mary's Church, Nantwich. Dating from around 1400 and portraying a fowl with a minister's face on its rear end, the image is said to have been carved by the craftsman in retaliation for not being paid by the vicar for his work.

Celebrating Twelfth Night with King Cake and Hot Punch

The sixth of January, also known as Epiphany (see CHRIST-MAS DINNER), is the the last day of the twelve days of Christmas. The evening before it is known as Twelfth Night. In many European countries, a special pastry or cake made with dried fruit, known as the **king cake**, is baked for the occasion. In France, for instance, this is called the *galette/gâteau des rois*, in Spain the *roscón des reyes*, and in Portugal the *bolo rei*. Traditionally, a bean is inserted—more likely a little plastic trinket these days—into the cake mix. The lucky person to come across the bean in their portion of cake is then crowned king or queen for the evening.

This calls to mind the Three Kings of the Nativity story, who arrived to pay their respects to the infant Jesus on the twelfth day after his birth, but the tradition is actually much older, predating Christianity itself. Twelfth Night used to mark the end of the winter festival that began at the end of October with the Celtic festival of Samhain (now Halloween) and the ancient Roman festival of Saturnalia. In the Celtic tradition, on the final day of the festival the world would turn upside down for the evening, presided over by the Lord of Misrule—now represented by the person who finds the bean in the cake. This topsy-turviness is reflected in Shakespeare's play *Twelfth Night* (1601) with Viola, one of the central characters, dressing as a man and the servant Malvolio believing that he can court a noblewoman, thanks to the machinations of Feste the clown, who presides over events as the mischievous Lord of Misrule.

Part of the Twelfth Night celebrations was the tradition of wassailing—going from house to house wishing the occupants well (a practice that evolved into going caroling) and in return receiving **wassail** (derived from Middle English *wæs hæil*, "be in good health!"), a hot, spiced PUNCH served in a special cup called a wassail bowl. Needless to say, the revellers would get increasingly the worse for wear as the evening progressed, which probably accounts for the lyrics of the sixteenth-century wassailing carol "We Wish You a Merry Christmas," in which the singers demand "figgy pudding" and "a cup of good cheer" and then insist:

> We won't go until we get some;
> We won't go until we get some;
> We won't go until we get some, so bring some out here!

Try singing that outside my house on a cold winter's night, dear singers. You will certainly get some.

14
The Dessert Cart

A Brief History of the Pie

Pavlova: The Cold Dessert That Inspired a Hot Debate

Peach Melba: The Dessert That Defrosted a Diva

Crêpes Suzette: Pancakes for a Prince?

Survival of the Sweetest: How Trifle
Outlived Its Evolutionary Rivals

Tarte Tatin: A Culinary Reversal of Fortune

Apple Brown Betty: One Dessert That
Definitely Didn't Get Lost in Translation

From Arab Delicacy to All-American Treat:
The Story of Ice Cream

In Remembrance of Cakes Past:
The Petite Madeleine

The Story of the Bun: Sally Lunn,
Chelsea, and Hot Cross

It's not improbable that a man may receive more solid satisfaction from pudding while he is alive than from praise after he is dead.

PROVERB

Ice cream is exquisite. What a pity it isn't illegal.

VOLTAIRE

A Brief History of the Pie

Pies are an essential part of the cuisine of central and northern Europe and occur elsewhere (such as North America) only as introduced dishes, probably spread by the Romans, who in turn pinched the idea from the ancient Greeks. Food historian Alan Davidson, in *The Penguin Companion to Food* (2002), suggests that the derivation of the word may be from "magpie," shortened to "pie." These birds are known to collect a variety of things, and it was an essential feature of the earliest pies that they contained a variety of ingredients. It's only been more recently that pies have contained one chief ingredient, such as **apple pie**.

The first pies as we'd recognize them were eaten by the nobility and were called "coffins" (which formerly just meant a container). Very large and filled with assorted meats in a sauce, they were baked like a modern casserole but using the crust itself as the pot. The tough (almost inedible) pastry, called "huff paste," was discarded after the filling had been eaten (rather like bread trenchers—see OPEN-FACED SANDWICH) or given to the servants. As time went by, pies became smaller and the pastry tastier (often enriched with butter), and they were no longer just the preserve of the aristocracy.

Humble pie is not a real dish, of course, but a type of apology in which the person apologizing usually has to accept some sort of humiliation in the process. The expression dates back to the Middle Ages and the banquets held after a long day hunting. During the feast the lord of the manor and his noble guests would expect to be served the finest cuts of venison, while the deer's entrails, or offal, known as "umble" or "numble" (from the French *nomble*), would be baked in a pie and served to lower-class folk, or perhaps to those who were out of favor with the lord. Hence a higher-class diner seated at the wrong end of the table (accidentally or as a deliberate snub) would be forced to eat **umble pie** and endure the consequent humiliation.

Pavlova: The Cold Dessert That Inspired a Hot Debate

Anna Pavlova (1881–1931) may well be the most famous ballerina in dance history, synonymous with one of ballet's most enduring roles, that of the Dying Swan, created for her while she was a principal dancer at the Imperial Russian Ballet. Pavlova fell in love with ballet when she was just eight years old after seeing a performance of *The Sleeping Beauty*. Her mother took her to audition for the Imperial Ballet School but, frail and small for her age, she wasn't finally accepted until three years later. Once there, however, she trained obsessively and with the help of extra tuition the tiny dancer graduated in 1899, at the age of eighteen.

Pavlova went from strength to strength, her debut performance in Pavel Gerdt's *False Dryads* earning her high praise, not least by one noted critic and historian who complimented her on her "natural ballon, lingering arabesques, and frail

femininity." It was this frail femininity coupled with a grace-
ful energy that led to her quickly becoming a favorite with
both the adoring public and ballet masters alike. She was also
the first ballerina in history to go on tour around the world,
even as far afield as New Zealand and Australia, where her
first appearance was described as the "Chief Event of 1926."

The public of both countries were enraptured. "She does
not dance, she soars as though she has wings," was how the
New Zealand press described her during that first tour, in
1926. "Exquisite Pavlova!" cried the Australians. On her second tour of the continent, in 1929, the Australians were so
excited that one reporter noted: "A symphony of silence! But
who, seeing the famous ballerina for the first time as she
stood on deck at Fremantle yesterday, could apply that
description. It was Babel itself."

It was in honor of Pavlova, and her visits to the Antipodes,
that the famous dish bearing her name was invented. Consisting of a wide disk of meringue covered in whipped cream
and fresh fruit, **pavlova** is so called because its built-up sides
are thought to resemble the frothy layers of a tutu, and the
strawberry and passion fruit slices thought to resemble the
rose decorations upon her outfit. The dish is said to have
been created in New Zealand, but the Australians disagree,
saying that it originated in their country. With numerous
claims and counterclaims on both sides, it's a culinary tug of
war that has persisted for many years.

According to the Australians, the pavlova first appeared in
1934, three years after the dancer's death. Mrs. Elizabeth Paxton, owner of the Esplanade Hotel in Perth, asked the head
chef, Bert Sasche, to devise something special for the menu.
After a month of experimenting, Sasche presented the now-
famous dessert to his boss with the words, according to Paxton
family legend, "It's as light as Pavlova," a clear reference to the

dancer who was once their guest. Sasche stood by this claim for the rest of his life, although he did admit that the dish wasn't entirely original, explaining in a magazine interview in 1973 that he had based it on an existing recipe. Indeed, it's possible that he may have seen a recipe for meringue cake that appeared on April 2, 1935, in *Women's Mirror*, submitted by a lady from New Zealand.

Meanwhile, Pavlova's biographer Keith Mooney supports the idea that the dish originated in New Zealand, claiming that it was the creation of a young chef at a hotel in Wellington who had fallen in love with the ballerina during her first tour in 1926. Since the publication of *Anna Pavlova: Her Life and Art* in 1982, Australian food historians have argued that while the dessert seems to have been invented in New Zealand, it was only named after her later, in Australia, as proven by Australian cookbooks, which didn't include pavlova until the 1940s.

And so the debate raged on, with each side refuting the other's claims, until 2008 and the publication by Dr. Helen Leach, a culinary expert at the University of Otago in New Zealand, of *The Pavlova Story: A Slice of New Zealand's Culinary History*. Since then, the Australians have gone a little quiet on the subject, as Leach, in her research for the book, managed to unearth evidence for a pavlova in a New Zealand women's magazine from 1929. She also discovered a recipe for the dish in the *Rangiora Mothers' Union Cookery Book*, a New Zealand publication of 1933, while Mrs. McKay's *Practical Home Cookery Book* of 1929 includes a recipe for three dozen "little pavlovas." So unless the Australians can come up with an earlier, printed recipe, then I'm afraid this debate appears to be over, sport.

The expression **as easy as pie**, meaning very easy indeed, is a curious one. Why should a pie be easy, after all? It seems that the ease of the pie is in the eating rather than the making of it, as in the similar expression **nice as pie**. Both originate in nineteenth-century America, where likening something to a particular pie is also archetypally American—**as American as apple pie**, in fact.

Something described as **pie in the sky** is essentially a good idea but unlikely to amount to anything in reality. The phrase comes from a trade union parody of the hymn "The Sweet By and By" that was often sung during the years of the Great Depression early in the twentieth century. The song was entitled "The Preacher and the Slave" and its chorus, goes like this:

> You will eat, bye and bye
> In that glorious land above the sky;
> Work and pray, live on hay,
> You'll get pie in the sky when you die.

And somehow that passed over into wider use, but don't ask how.

Moving back across the Atlantic, to have **a finger in every pie** is an expression commonly used to describe a person who has an interest in many things, especially business-related. It would be easier to understand if the phrase read "a finger in *making* every pie," which would rid us of the image of somebody going around poking their finger into other people's peach crumble, thereby suggesting an interfering meddler. The expression has been in use for over four hundred years and is applied to anybody with wide and varied business interests. It is also used by some people to describe themselves in an attempt to appear mysterious and interesting when in fact they've probably never had their finger in anybody's pie.

Peach Melba: The Dessert That Defrosted a Diva

Auguste Escoffier (1846–1935) was a French chef, restaurateur, and writer, a key figure in the development of modern French cuisine. In the 1880s, he formed a partnership with the equally celebrated César Ritz (founder of the Ritz Hotel in London), the two of them being called upon by Richard D'Oyly Carte (see SOLE VÉRONIQUE) to run the Savoy Hotel, where Escoffier devised some of his most famous dishes. Aside from being the most respected chef in London during the 1890s, Escoffier was also an avid opera fan, and legend has it that he forged a friendship with one of the greatest opera singers of her era, Dame Nellie Melba (1861–1931), when she was staying at the Savoy.

One evening in 1893, the Australian singer, and reputed

drama queen extraordinaire, remarked to Escoffier that she loved ice cream but was unable to eat it in case it froze her vocal cords. Never averse to a challenge, the chef went straight to his kitchen and set about experimenting with ICE CREAM mixed with different types of fruit and sauces, in the hope that these might render the dish less chilly. He soon hit upon his favorite combination, peaches and vanilla ice cream smothered in raspberry sauce (although alternative versions of the story ascribe the sauce to a later version of the dish). In a dramatic flourish, the chef later presented his new creation in an ice sculpture of a swan, in reference to *Lohengrin* and its story of the Swan Knight. Melba was so enchanted by the dish that she was soon demanding it at restaurants and hotels the world over. Since then, **peach Melba** has proved such a hit that January 13 has been declared National Peach Melba Day. (See also MELBA TOAST for another dish inspired by the diva.)

Crêpes Suzette: Pancakes for a Prince?

Like many of the world's best dishes, **crêpes Suzette**— pancakes covered in Grand Marnier and flambéed—was created by accident at the Café de Paris in Monte Carlo. During a stay in 1895, the notorious womanizer the Prince of Wales was dining with one of his mistresses when a fourteen-year-old waiter, Henri Charpentier (1880–1961), made a mistake as he prepared the princely plateful. Charpentier described the incident himself in his autobiography, *Life à la Henri*, published during the 1940s:

> It was by accident as I worked in front of a chafing dish that the cordials caught fire. I thought it was ruined. The Prince and his friends were waiting. How could I begin it all over? So I tasted it and it was, I thought, the most delicious melody of sweet flavors I had ever tasted, and I still think so. That accident of the flame was precisely what was needed to bring all those various instruments into one harmony of taste . . . He ate the pancakes with a fork but used a spoon to capture the remaining syrup. When he asked me for the name of what he had eaten with such relish, I told him it was to be called Crêpes au Prince. The Prince recognized . . . that this was a compliment designed for him, but he protested with mock ferocity that there was a lady present. She was alert and rose to her feet and holding her little skirt wide with her hands she made a curtsy. "Will you," said His Majesty, "change Crêpes au Prince to Crêpes Suzette?" Thus was born and baptized this confection, one taste of which, I believe, would reform a cannibal into a civilized gentleman. The following day I received a present from the Prince, a jeweled ring, a panama hat, and a cane.

Survival of the Sweetest: How Trifle Outlived Its Evolutionary Rivals

Hedgehog pudding, tipsy cake, tansy, syllabub, flummery, junket, trifle: the only popular survivor of these favorites of the eighteenth-century banquet today is the rich cold dessert known as **trifle**. The word comes from the old French term *trufle*, meaning something whimsical or of little consequence. The modern trifle consists of a thin layer of bread soaked in "sack" (dry white wine) and covered in custard flavored with rose water.

By the middle of the eighteenth century, trifles had expanded to absorb macaroons soaked in sweet wine, covered with custard, and topped with syllabub (milk or cream sweetened with sugar and lightly curdled with wine), this last addition eventually replaced with whipped cream. At this point, trifle shared the culinary limelight with a number of similar dishes, including the aforementioned tipsy cake (soaked in alcohol, surrounded by custard or syllabub, and dotted all over with slivered almonds) and hedgehog pudding (a variation on tipsy cake, with the almonds poking out like spines). But the trifle eventually upstaged its rivals, absorbing the almonds as decoration on top of the syllabub/whipped cream.

How trifle became a lastingly popular dessert may well be for reasons of thrift: it offered a delicious way to use up stale cake, custard, and fruit (a much later stage in the evolution of the trifle) plus any other leftovers from a week's worth of desserts. This may also be why the Italian version is jokingly called *zuppa inglese* (English soup), because the British, who created the dish, were renowned in their country for two things: recycling all leftovers into soup for the next day (see MULLIGATAWNY); and an obsessive love of dessert.

Tarte Tatin: A Culinary Reversal of Fortune

Most cultures have their own recipe for apple pie. In America it has even become part of the national identity, with the saying "as American as apple pie" (see page 241). But the French version, the **tarte Tatin**, is commonly recognized as one of the best in the world. And like CREPES SUZETTE, it was invented by accident. The Hôtel Tatin in Lamotte-Beuvron, France, was run by a pair of unmarried sisters, Stéphanie and Caroline Tatin, during the late 1800s. Usually everything ran very smoothly, but, one day, the apples for a traditional pie were left cooking in sugar and butter for too long, and burned. Stéphanie Tatin, who was in charge of the kitchen, tried to save the dish by pressing a disc of pastry on top of the apples and putting the pan in the oven. She then turned the contents of the pan out onto a plate, creating a sort of upside-down tart in the process (except that now it was the right way up, of course). To the sisters' amazement, the hotel patrons raved about the resulting dish, with its topping of buttery, caramelized apples, and a classic was born, ensuring fabulous advertising for the hotel forever after.

Tarte Tatin immediately became a signature dish of the Hôtel Tatin, and the recipe, and its unusual cooking technique, soon spread throughout the surrounding Sologne region. But it became an international sensation when Louis Vaudable, the legendary owner of Maxim's Restaurant in Paris, was served a slice when traveling through the area. He immediately made the tart a permanent fixture on the menu of his restaurant, where it is still served to this day.

Apple Brown Betty: One Dessert That Definitely Didn't Get Lost in Translation

The early European settlers of America were very good at improvization, but they had to be. In the absence of key ingredients and suitable cooking apparatus, they were obliged to use whatever was available. Their attempts to cook their favorite steamed sweets resulted in a series of sloppier (but very tasty) desserts, all similar to crisps. The settlers definitely had a sense of humor about the aesthetic failings of their new dishes: calling one "slump" was in direct reference to how the traditional dessert reacted to their more basic cooking apparatus, and christening another "cobbler" reflected how they had had to cobble ingredients together to make the dish. Yet they were so fond of these dishes that they often served them for breakfast, or even as the first course for dinner. It was not until the late nineteenth century that they became primarily desserts.

One favorite of these baked desserts was the **apple brown betty**, which became very popular during the Civil War (1861–5). It consisted of alternate layers of thinly sliced apples and breadcrumbs, which meant that it was easy to prepare on the move and robust enough not to fall apart. The first mention in print was in the *Yale Literary Magazine* in 1864 where brown betties appeared on a list with coffee, tea, and pies as items to be given up during military training. On Monday, July 11, 1938, the *Daily Times* newspaper in Rochester, New York, published a recipe for brown betties, suggesting they were named after a young English lass called Betty Brown, who had emigrated to North America during the early 1800s. But the real reason behind the name may well be yet another joke from the settlers: apple brown betty was their rather more down-to-earth version of the European favorite **apple charlotte** . . .

If someone gets their **just deserts**, it is generally thought that they had what was coming to them; they got what they deserved. The confusion over the origins of this phrase lies in the spelling of "deserts." It looks like the word that means a vast sandy place in Egypt, but sounds like that pie and ice cream we might have after dinner, which is why the phrase is often explained as "Well, he deserved a pudding like that after what he did." But this is wrong. The *Concise Oxford Dictionary* gives three definitions for the word "desert": (1) to "callously or treacherously abandon"; (2) "a waterless, desolate area of land with little or no vegetation, typically covered with sand"; and (3) "a person's worthiness or entitlement to reward or punishment." It is this third definition that explains the phrase "just deserts," meaning an appropriate reward or (more usually) punishment for someone's actions, and nothing at all to do with pie or indeed any other kind of dessert, just or otherwise.

From Arab Delicacy to All-American Treat: The Story of Ice Cream

Today we take it for granted, but in the days before refrigeration, the possession of ice in hot climates or throughout the summer was a luxury that could only be afforded by the very rich. From ancient times, special buildings known as ice houses were contructed to store ice and snow gathered during the winter, keeping it frozen during the blazing summer months. The Persians introduced these, and it was they who, around 400 BC, first put the ice to culinary use. Mixing ice with rose water, saffron, and fruit, they made a chilled dessert that became the precursor of the **Italian ice** or **sorbet**. (They also made fruit drinks chilled with snow called "sherbets," from which the word "sorbet" derives.) The Romans also stored ice and snow, which they, too, used for making iced drinks and desserts. Such was his passion for these that, in AD 62, the emperor Nero, famed for his extravagance, sent slaves to the Apennine Mountains to collect snow for an iced dish flavored with honey and nuts. It was the Arabs who first made ices into a dairy dessert, sweetening the milky liquid with sugar rather than fruit juices to create an early form of **ice cream** that became very popular in Baghdad, Damascus, and Cairo.

The Chinese may very well have invented their own prototypes of sorbet and ice cream at the same time as the Persians and Arabs (a frozen mixture of milk and rice was reputedly used in China around 200 BC), but the story that, like PASTA, the recipes and techniques were brought back to Italy by Marco Polo is very unlikely to be true. What is irrefutably the case is that, by the sixteenth century, Italy had become the home of the frozen dessert, which Catherine de Médicis then introduced to France via her team of Italian chefs (see EGGS FLORENTINE). But while Europe preferred Italian ices, the perfecting of ice cream was down to the English, who were much more interested in a frozen version of their favorite thick, rich custards. The first recorded English use of the word dates back to 1672, where it is listed as a key dessert for special occasions, and the first recipe to 1718. From the mid-eighteenth century onward, while still an expensive delicacy, ice cream began to appear more frequently in cookbooks. Hannah Glasse included a recipe in her 1751 edition of *The Art of*

Cookery, for instance, while in 1768 *L'Art de bien faire les glaces d'office*, a work entirely devoted to the subject, was published in France.

Ice cream was introduced to America by Quaker colonists, who brought their ice cream recipes with them. Benjamin Franklin, George Washington, and Thomas Jefferson were all known to have been fans of the dish. It took American energy and egalitarianism to realize the full potential of ice cream, and from the first time it was formally served at a banquet in 1744, they proceeded to make it their national dish. Confectioners sold ice cream at their shops in New York and other cities during the colonial era. This was received so enthusiastically that, on both sides of the Atlantic, ice cream came to be regarded as an entirely American concoction, so much so that in museums and antique shops early ice cream makers and molds from Europe were mislabeled as American.

ICE CREAM SODAS AND SUNDAES

Two variations of ice cream, the **ice cream soda** and the **ice cream sundae**, are both genuinely all-American creations, however. The first is believed to have been the invention of a Philadelphia soda vendor, Robert M. Green, in 1874. According to the story, it was a particularly hot day and Green, having run out of ice for the drinks he was selling, tried substituting it with vanilla ice cream from a neighboring vendor. His new creation caught on, and the drink sold so well that it soon became the national institution that it is today. Meanwhile, Green was so proud of his invention that he instructed in his will that the words "Originator of the Ice Cream Soda" be carved on his tombstone.

The ice cream sundae emerged slightly later, reputedly the creation of two competing ice cream parlor owners in Wisconsin, although there are rival claims from elsewhere in America. Ed Berners in Two Rivers discovered almost by accident in 1881 that the chocolate sauce he used for making sodas made a delicious topping for ice cream, and went on to create a number of ice-cream-and-sauce combinations, which he called the Flora Dora, the Mudscow, and the Chocolate Peany. But it was George Giffy, in nearby Manitowoc, who hit on a name that stuck. He started serving these special ice creams to parishioners after church on Sundays. Then one weekday a little girl ordered a dish of ice cream "with stuff on it." On being told that Giffy only served it on Sundays, the child was supposed to have replied: "Why, then it must be Sunday, for that's the kind of ice cream I want!" Keen to avert the brewing tantrum, Giffy quickly made the dish for her and from then on called it a "Sunday."

To **take the cake** is an expression meaning to be outrageous enough to deserve merit. A stunt pilot or racing driver, for example, might "take the cake" for his audacity. It has been recorded that this phrase originated in the late nineteenth century among black slaves working on southern plantations. It seems they devised a game whereby couples would parade arm in arm around a barn and were judged by the others on the style and grace of their walk. The winning couple would be given a cake as a prize, and the most flamboyant and entertaining of them could expect to hear cries of "they take the cake." This pastime was known as the **cakewalk**, which is also a well-known expression for something that is easy to achieve.

However, it is quite possible that the root of this expression goes back much earlier, to the Bible in fact. As missionaries converted large parts of Africa to Christianity, teaching from the Bible became widespread. For most inhabitants of the region, it was likely to have been the only book they had ever read; thus its influence was profound. There is one story, for instance, telling how a biblical knight would be rewarded with a cake made of toasted cereal, sweetened with honey, if he was judged the most successful knight either in battle or in the workplace. There is strong evidence to suggest that African Americans adopted this reward after learning about the tale.

In Remembrance of Cakes Past: The Petite Madeleine

She sent out for one of those short, plump little cakes called "petites madeleines," which look as though they had been moulded in the fluted scallop of a pilgrim's shell. And soon, mechanically, weary after a dull day with the prospect of a depressing morrow, I raised to my lips a spoonful of the tea in which I had soaked a morsel of the cake. No sooner had the warm liquid, and the crumbs with it, touched my palate than a shudder ran through my whole body, and I stopped, intent upon the extraordinary changes that were taking place . . . at once the vicissitudes of life had become indifferent to me, its disasters innocuous, its brevity illusory . . .

Small sponge cakes baked in distinctive shell-shaped molds, **madeleines** are now among the most recognizable cakes in the world thanks to Marcel Proust (1871–1922) and his *In Search of Lost Time*. Eating a madeleine (in the passage from the book quoted above) sends the narrator off on a (very) long journey into involuntary memory. But who was the original Madeleine that they were named after? Some sources suggest that she was a French pastry chef working for the deposed king of Poland, Stanisław Leszczyński. Forced by an assassination attempt to seek exile in France, he and his family moved to the Château de Commercy in the commune of Commercy in northeastern France. When in 1755 Madeleine Paulmier became his pastry chef, she supposedly invented the cake to cheer up the exiled king.

But the cakes are much more likely to be named after a very different Madeleine, for Madeleine is also the French name for Mary Magdalen, the former prostitute and follower of Jesus. Several orders of nuns have taken her name and that, twinned with the cake's distinctive scallop-shell shape (the traditional symbol of a Catholic pilgrim, as Proust himself points out above), would suggest that the cakes were originally baked with a more religious purpose in mind, perhaps to remind those who ate them that while, like Mary/Madeleine herself, we are all sinners, we are also pilgrims on a hopeful journey to find God.

The Story of the Bun: Sally Lunn, Chelsea, and Hot Cross

While in America, **bun** is a generic name for a bread roll of some kind, either sweet or savory, British buns are much sweeter and richer. The word has been used since at least the fifteenth century and is derived from the French *bugne* or "swelling," referring to its bulging shape. There are many kinds of buns. Here are three of the most interesting.

THE SALLY LUNN

During the seventeenth century, the Protestant Huguenots were persecuted by the Catholic Church (see HOLLANDAISE SAUCE and MORNAY SAUCE) and many caught the boat to England. The Huguenots were respected as skilled lace makers, weavers, and merchants, mainly specializing in silk. And they soon became an important part of English society at a time when the English were emerging from the cheerless grip of Oliver Cromwell's Puritan regime (1649–60). The Huguenots wielded vast influence in terms of business, finance, and physical support for the new monarchy, restored under Charles II (although many Huguenots were to later fight for the Protestant William of Orange against the English king during the Glorious Revolution of 1688, which must have made Charles, who had invited them in the first place, turn in his grave).

The influence of the Huguenots also extended to British cuisine. One of the new settlers was a pretty young girl called Solange Luyon, who relocated to Bath in Somerset and soon found work at a bakery. Almost immediately she began baking a light, round teacake that became the talk of the town as locals would line up at breakfast time for one of "Sollie's" cakes. Bath and nearby Bristol both being a hub for travelers, word soon got around and the anglicized **Sally Lunn bun** became hugely popular throughout Georgian England. Today the original recipe is passed along with the deeds to the bakery, now known as Sally Lunn's and thought to be the oldest house in Bath. Visitors can still buy a Sally Lunn bun at the tea shop/museum, safe in the knowledge that some things will never change.

THE CHELSEA BUN

One of the most popular buns in England, the **Chelsea bun** was created and sold exclusively at the Chelsea Bun House in Pimlico, London, from the beginning of the 1700s. A glazed square bun made from a spiral of dough flavored with lemon peel, cinnamon, and other spices, it was popular with royals and commoners alike. Mad King George III (1738–1820) was a regular customer, often popping in for a Chelsea bun on his way from the palace to the nearby Pleasure Gardens, and the bakery became unofficially known as the Royal Bun House. Despite the original business closing in 1840 when the building was knocked down, the legend of the Chelsea Bun House lived on, and its replacement, the Real Old Chelsea Bun House (which, of course, it wasn't), proved to be equally popular.

The bakery and its famous buns were subsequently commemorated in literature. In 1840 (the year of its closure), Charles Dickens drew attention to the bakery in *Barnaby Rudge*, his account of the Gordon Riots (1780), describing in one passage how the Royal East London Volunteers marched in "glittering order to the Chelsea Bun House and then regaled in the adjacent taverns until dark." In 1855, Anne Manning, prolific author of some fifty-one works, called one of her novels *The Old Chelsea Bun House: A Tale of the Last Century*, while in one of his short stories from *A Tangled Tale* (1880), Lewis Carroll has one of his characters exclaim: "Give her a Chelsea bun, miss! That's what most young ladies like best!" The man, a street hawker with a "rich and musical" voice, goes on to display his wares:

> the speaker dexterously whipped back the snowy cloth
> that covered his basket, and disclosed a tempting array
> of the familiar square buns, joined together in rows,
> richly egged and browned and glistening in the sun.

Needless to say, the young lady in question is sorely tempted, but gets whisked away by her fierce aunt before she can succumb.

THE HOT CROSS BUN

For many people the **hot cross bun** epitomizes Easter, particularly Good Friday and the crucifixion of Jesus Christ, in commemoration of which the bun is said to have been created. According to Elizabeth David in *English Bread and Yeast Cookery* (1977), sweet, spiced buns have been popular since Tudor times but were permitted only on special occasions. In 1592, during the reign of Queen Elizabeth I, the following decree was issued by the London Clerk of the Markets:

> That no bakers, etc, at any time, or times hereafter, may make, utter or sell by retail within or without their houses, unto any of the Queen's subjects any spice cakes, buns, biscuits, or any other spice bread (being bread out of size and not by law allowed) except it be at burials, or on the Friday before Easter, or at Christmas, upon pain of forfeiture of all such spiced bread to the poor.

It is not known exactly why such a decree should have been made, but that seems to be when the tradition for spiced buns on Good Friday began, although the first recorded use of the term "hot cross bun" wasn't until 1733. The custom was clearly well established later in the century, however, such that by 1791 James Boswell was referring to it in his *Life of Samuel Johnson*, recalling how in 1773 that "being Good Friday I breakfasted with him [Johnson] and Hot Cross Buns."

The tradition of eating special food at Easter actually goes back much further, to the time of the Anglo-Saxons, who worshipped a goddess of the dawn, Eostre, from whom the words "east" and "Easter" derive. It's believed that the Saxons offered small cakes to the goddess on her feast day at the spring equinox, a custom going back to the ancient Greeks and Romans, who both had traditional spring festivals involving bread offerings to their gods.

These days hot cross buns are sold all the year round,

thanks to the unstoppable rise of the supermarket. However, there is one place in Britain where spiced buns are still associated with special days of celebration, albeit in rather a strange way. In Abingdon in Oxfordshire, to mark important events such as coronations and royal jubilees, local dignitaries all assemble on the roof of the county hall and pelt buns at the populace assembled in the market square below. (Needless to say, everyone immediately scrambles for them and a literal bun fight ensues—see below.) The county hall, now a museum, holds a collection of buns, dried and varnished, that have been thrown through the ages. Not sure I'd care to be on the receiving end of one of those.

The term **bun fight** is an expression, used tongue in cheek, for any grand occasion at which people dress up and food is served. Focusing on the "fight" element, the term is also used in a rather different sense, to mean a heated exchange, generally one that has no real importance except to the participants—**a storm in a teacup**, you might otherwise say (using another teatime analogy). The term is believed to go back to the nineteenth century and the elaborate AFTERNOON TEAS that used to be served in well-to-do Victorian households. These meals traditionally consisted of a whole range of buns, scones, and teacakes—all conveniently missile-shaped. Hence, if the diners were children, it's easy to see how things might degenerate if Nanny lost control.

15
The Cheese Course

What Was Little Miss Muffet Eating?

Brie: Blessed Are the Cheesemakers

Parmesan: Much Admired

Fondue: The Cheesy Alpine Classic

Defining Cheddar: Hard Cheese to the
Rest of the World

The Ancient Art of Making Cheese into a Cake

Cheese Rolling: An Energetic Way to
Serve Double Gloucester

A Cracker to Accompany the Cheese

I saw a figure leap with great rapidity behind the trunk of a pine . . .

"Who are you?" I asked.

"Ben Gunn," he answered, and his voice sounded awkward, like a rusty lock. "I'm poor Ben Gunn, I am; and I haven't spoke with a Christian these three years . . . But, mate, my heart is sore for Christian diet. You mightn't happen to have a piece of cheese about you, now? No? Well, many's the long night I've dreamed of cheese—toasted, mostly—and woke up again, and here I were."

ROBERT LOUIS STEVENSON, *Treasure Island*

What Was Little Miss Muffet Eating?

A major change brought by the development of organized farming around 7000 BC was that animals were suddenly no longer seen merely in terms of their meat. And as soon as humans began to milk their domesticated animals, the issue of how to preserve this delicious, nutritious but rapidly rancid liquid became a pressing concern. It's likely the earliest type of cheese was a form of sour milk, a simple result of the observation that milk left in a container turned solid, especially in hot temperatures. However, according to one widely told legend, **cheese** was an accidental discovery, similar to that of STEAK TARTARE and originating in the same part of the world, Central Asia. To sustain himself on a long journey across the desert, a nomad once filled his saddlebag with milk, tying it to his saddle. After several hours of galloping in the hot sun, he stopped to quench his thirst, only to find the milk had separated into a thin, sour watery liquid and solid white lumps. The rennet in the sheep's stomach, from which the saddlebag was made, had caused the milk to set, turning it into a form of cheese. Otherwise known as **curds and whey**, this is the very snack Little Miss Muffet was eating when she sat down on her nursery rhyme tuffet. And it is this that provides the basis for all our favorite cheeses.

The modern type of cheese that most resembles this basic early form is **cottage cheese**. It became a popular staple in Europe in the late Middle Ages, when rural workers became expert in deriving nourishment from almost anything. And from a nutritional point of view, cheese is a most valuable food, concentrating as it does most of the nourishment of the milk: the solids extracted from milk to make cheese contain virtually all of the fat, vitamins, and proteins. The workers would salvage any leftovers from cheese and butter making, which they took home and turned into a cheese that was so simple to create that it could easily be made in any dwelling, however humble or poorly equipped. The technique for making cottage (or cottager's) cheese was brought by early European settlers to America, where it also went by a rather less appetizing name, as indicated in *The Dictionary of Americanisms* (1848): "Smear-Case is a preparation of milk made to be spread onto bread, hence its name but otherwise known as Cottage Cheese." Deriving from the German *Schmierkäse* ("spreadable cheese"), **smearcase** reflected the mix of nationalities among the colonists. But as America's many German settlers became increasingly anglicized, the name was eventually dropped in favor of "cottage cheese." The Amish—who trace a direct line to their Swiss forefathers and continue to speak a form of German—remain resistant to all forms of anglicization and modernization, and their recipe for CHEESE-CAKE is still called **smearcase cake**.

Brie: Blessed Are the Cheesemakers

In Homer's *Odyssey*, Circe when trying to seduce Odysseus serves him cheese. The Greeks and Romans were obsessed with cheese and cheese-making features in many of their writings and mosaics. By AD 300, cheese trade and export was well under way along the Mediterranean seaboard and throughout Europe. But when the Roman Empire fell to the Barbarians (around AD 410), the Dark Ages began and cheese all but disappeared.

Luckily for us, the early Christian Church, as we've seen with CHRISTMAS DINNER, had a great eye for the most attractive parts of pagan life, and eventually monks in early monasteries all around Europe revived the practice of cheese making. Removed from the commercial pressures of the outside world, monasteries offered great opportunities for innovation, and the monks greatly improved techniques for cheese ripening and aging. One type to emerge during these times was **Brie**, the famous soft French cheese with its distinctive doughy white crust. Originating in the Brie region of northern France around 770, it is the subject of a well-known legend. According to a ninth-century biography of the first Holy Roman Emperor, Charlemagne (742–814), who conquered and Christianized vast tracts of Dark Age Europe, he was traveling through the region and stopped at a bishop's residence for dinner.

> Now on that day, being [Friday], he was not willing to eat the flesh of beast or bird; and the bishop, being by reason of the nature of the place unable to procure fish upon the sudden, ordered some excellent cheese, rich and creamy, to be placed before him. Charles . . . required no better fare: but taking up his knife cut off the skin, which he thought unsavoury, and fell to on the white of the cheese. Thereupon the bishop, who was standing near like a servant, drew close and said: "Why do you do that, lord emperor? You are throwing away the very best part." Then Charles . . . on the persuasion of the bishop put a piece of the skin in his mouth, and slowly ate it and swallowed it like butter. Then, approving the advice of the bishop, he said: "Very true, my good host," and added: "Be sure to send me every year two cart-loads of just such cheeses."

For his pains, the bishop was awarded an "excellent estate" to add to the Church lands, while Brie went on to become one of the most defining French cheeses.

Big cheese is a colloquial expression for the most important person. During the early nineteenth century, "cheese" was a common slang term used by Londoners to describe anything genuine or popular. John Camden Hotten's *Slang Dictionary*, first published in 1863, describes "cheese" as "anything good, first rate, genuine and pleasant." Used in this sense, the word has nothing to do with the dairy product but appears to have been a corruption of the Persian word *chiz*, meaning "item" or "thing." As Sir Henry Yule explains in *Hobson-Jobson*, the famous Anglo-Indian dictionary, *chiz* was commonly used by Anglo-Indians in the form "real *chiz*," to describe something (or someone) that was the best of its kind. In America in the early twentieth century, this phrase was corrupted further to "big cheese," following on from a whole range of "big" phrases describing the best of something, including **big fish**, **big bug**, and **big banana**. The phrase is not entirely complimentary, however, with overtones of other "cheese" expressions, such as **cheesed off** (to be annoyed) and **cheesy** (cheap or inauthentic). Deriving perhaps from the strong odor of the actual substance, "cheesy" could equally have evolved as an ironic application of *chiz* ("chizzy") to indicate something showy and tasteless.

Parmesan: Much Admired

There is a mountain in Boccaccio's *Decameron* that is made entirely of grated **Parmesan**, on which there live people who do nothing but make MACARONI and RAVIOLI. Made in Italy from the Middle Ages, chiefly in the area of Parma (from which its name derives), Parmesan was the favorite cheese of both Napoleon and Samuel Pepys, who famously buried his Parmesan, "as well as [his] wine and some other things," in order to preserve it from the ravages of the Great Fire of London in 1666. The playwright Molière (1622–73), suddenly stricken by a fatal illness, waved aside the conventional bowl of medicinal broth, and called for Parmesan, which he devoured with such enthusiasm that there were cheese crumbs all over his deathbed. Although it failed to revive him, Parmesan had and still has a reputation as being good for the health—as well as being highly nutritious, its long aging process makes it easy to digest and it is believed to encourage the development of "friendly" bacteria in the gut.

Fondue: The Cheesy Alpine Classic

Cheese fondue was originally a Swiss peasant recipe: up in the Alps the peasants relied very heavily on the produce of their herds and on cheese in particular. Fondue offered a clever one-pot cooking method for using up scraps of cheese and bits of stale bread—for dipping in the cheese sauce once it had been made. The word derives from the French verb *fondre* ("to melt"), and simply means "melted." Most Swiss would agree that a proper fondue is made with a blend of cheeses—hard Gruyère with a semi-hard cheese like Emmental or raclette—plus white wine, a little brandy, a spoonful of flour to prevent curdling, and a sprinkling of salt, pepper, and nutmeg. However, the dish might have remained an overlooked regional delicacy if it were not for the intervention of French gastronome and cheese enthusiast Jean Anthelme Brillat-Savarin (1755–1826). His classic book *The Physiology of Taste* (published in 1825, two months before his death) has a rather strange entry on fondue, describing it as "a soup . . . that consists of frying eggs in cheese in proportions revealed by experience"—a recipe that incidentally has been condemned by Swiss authorities as being for scrambled eggs with cheese rather than a true fondue. Nevertheless, the dish became so popular that it was picked up and highly recommended by Mrs. Beeton in her *Book of Household Management* in 1861. Such was his passion for cheese that Brillat-Savarin has one named after him—a very creamy, Brie-like soft cheese from Normandy. And it was he who came up with the unforgettable saying that "a dinner without cheese was like a beautiful woman with only one eye."

To **grin like a Cheshire cat** means that you are feeling extremely pleased with yourself and therefore smiling very broadly indeed. It's an expression that immediately calls to mind the Cheshire Cat in Lewis Carroll's *Alice's Adventures in Wonderland* (1865), in which the cat, perched on a branch, gradually disappears until only its grin is visible. But where did Carroll get the inspiration for his grinning feline? There are suggestions that the idea may have come from a carving of a cat on St. Wilfrid's Church tower in Grappenhall, a village near Daresbury, Cheshire, in northwest England where the author was born. Or that it may relate to the image of a cat or lion with a strange smile said to have appeared on the coat of arms of a prominent Cheshire family, the Grosvenors. If that's the case, then other people must have been similarly inspired, as the expression appears in a much older work, *The Classical Dictionary of the Vulgar Tongue* (1788) by Francis Grose, which contains the entry: "He grins like a Cheshire cat; said of anyone who shows his teeth and gums in laughing." Another suggestion connects the phrase with **Cheshire cheese**, which, it is believed, used to be sold molded in the shape of a cat that looked as though it was grinning—no doubt having seen off a few mice keen to sink their teeth into the cheese. As bits of the cheese were cut off the "body" of the cat, only its head would remain, just like that of its fictional counterpart.

Defining Cheddar: Hard Cheese to the Rest of the World

Originally from the village of Cheddar in Somerset, England, **Cheddar cheese** has been produced since at least 1170, when the records of King Henry II (1133–89) reveal that he ordered 10,500 pounds of the cheese to be sent to him in London. Going forward a few centuries, the man credited with having invented the "defining formula" for it, and hence regarded as the "father of Cheddar cheese," was dairyman Joseph Harding (1805–76). It was he who introduced a more scientific approach to the process of cheese making, insisting on strict hygiene and temperature control, techniques that form the basis for commercial cheese making today. Indeed, such was his faith in his production process that he would say: "Cheese is not made in the field, nor in the byre, nor even in the cow; it is made in the dairy."

Harding was then consulted by cheese makers from America, who took his ideas with them across the Atlantic, and his techniques were adopted by other countries, too; hence a Cheddar-like cheese is produced in every corner of the globe. Cheese calling itself "Cheddar" is made in a multitude of places, although to be a true Cheddar, it traditionally had to be made within thirty miles of Wells Cathedral in Somerset. As with PARMESAN, the European Union has granted Cheddar a "protected designation of origin" status whereby only

West Country Farmhouse Cheddar is officially recognized, a label that can be applied only to the traditionally made product of four designated English counties: Dorset, Somerset, Devon, and Cornwall. Any other Cheddar cheese you come across (and supermarkets are full of them) is simply not authentic. So now you know.

The Ancient Art of Making Cheese into a Cake

The ancient Greeks lived on a frugal diet of wheat, olive oil, and wine, so it's easy to see where their obsession with cheese came from. They gave it to their children as a treat—"little cheese" was a special term of endearment. Their earliest cheese was a simple sheep's milk cheese that they stored in brine to save it from the blistering summer heat. Still a staple of the Greek diet, **feta** has been produced for centuries, although its name, derived from the Italian word *fetta*, or "slice," didn't become current until the seventeenth century. The blandness of feta makes it a highly versatile cheese, delicious in both savory and sweet dishes, including **cheesecake**, which also dates back to antiquity—made by the ancient Greeks and served on special occasions. Historians believe that it was even served to the athletes during the first Olympic Games in 776 BC, presumably as part of the athletes' dietary regime, which consisted chiefly of cheese.

Wedding cakes of that era were almost invariably made with cheese, while at Argos it was customary for the bride to bring little cheesecakes covered in honey for serving to the bride-groom's friends. The Romans were quick to pick up on the Greek dish, the earliest mention appearing in Cato the Elder's *De agri cultura* ("On Farming") around 160 BC, in which the author describes making a cake (*libum*) closely resembling the cheesecake of today. So the next time you eat a slice (*fetta*) of cheesecake, pause for a moment to think just how long people have been enjoying them.

Cheese Rolling: An Energetic Way to Serve Double Gloucester

Every year, on the spring bank holiday, the good folk of the village of Brockworth near Gloucester in southwest England hold a contest at Cooper's Hill, one that began as a small local festival and grew into a much publicized event attended by thousands of visitors from all over the world. Nobody remembers exactly how or why it started or what inspired the villagers to gather at the top of the hill and roll a large cheese down the steep, uneven slope and then go charging after it at breakneck speed to see who can reach the bottom first. The cheese in question is **Double Gloucester**, the locally produced variety of hard cheese that is typically manufactured in large cylindrical blocks. After rolling down the hill, this is awarded to the first contestant over the line. Ideally, it would be awarded to the person who catches it, but as the cheese can reach speeds of up to seventy miles an hour, this is perhaps a tall order. Needless to say, injuries are commonplace and the seven-pound cheese frequently strays offline and flattens an unsuspecting spectator. Even so, each year hundreds of people take part, often after discussing tactics in the nearby Cheese Rollers public house, considered by many to be responsible for much of the "over-enthusiasm" among competitors and for the need to position an ambulance at the bottom of the hill.

The Cooper's Hill Cheese Rolling and Wake (to give the contest its full title) is known to have been an established event as far back as the early 1800s. And it may go back further—to Roman times or beyond, perhaps as part of a pagan fertility ritual (hence the modern festival taking place on a spring holiday). During the food rationing of World War II, a wooden substitute was used, with a small wedge of cheese secured inside, just to keep the competition, as well as the cheese, rolling on from year to year.

To sum up the event, it appears to consist of a bunch of young men throwing themselves off a steep hill after a run-away cheese and racing each other to the emergency room. And quite why anybody would want to eat cheese that has careened down Cooper's Hill at speeds approaching the national limit is beyond me, especially if it drew the blood of an unsuspecting bystander along the way.

A Cracker to Accompany the Cheese

Good cheese needs something to show it off to best advantage, like the frame around a painting. Hence, at the end of a meal, cheese is frequently served with crackers, usually quite plain, in order to complement its creamy richness. One of the most familiar kind are **water crackers**, thin and hard with a flaky texture and golden brown bubbles all over the surface. Made using only flour and water, with no fat, they are baked in a very hot oven to create their distinctive bubbly brown surface. What may amaze the hosts of smart dinner parties serving them up with a platter of choice cheeses is that they are the descendants of SHIP'S BISCUIT, the detested and notoriously weevil-ridden staple diet of sailors until the twentieth century. Originally produced in the nineteenth century, they became known as "water crackers" in America due to the crackling sound they made during baking.

The final item in this selection is not strictly a cracker, although it is often served with cheese. Buoyed by his success with PEACH MELBA, and his growing friendship with Dame Nellie, Auguste Escoffier came up with another dish in her honor. During her stay at the Savoy Hotel, the singer was complaining of feeling ill one morning, apparently unable to eat her breakfast TOAST. Escoffier, who had been standing by her table, quickly took a sharp knife and—despite what must have been an obvious temptation to anyone in the company of a whining diva—applied it to the toast instead of the singer herself. He carefully sliced the toast through the middle, producing two thinner pieces that were easier for the great lady to swallow. And only half as fattening, which went down well with the singer, who was always trying to lose weight. Ever since that morning at the Savoy Hotel in 1897, **Melba toast** has gained in popularity, especially when it was discovered that it made the perfect accompaniment for soup or pâté, not to mention cheese.

Further Reading

Blake, Anthony, and Crewe, Quentin, *Great Chefs of France* (H. N. Abrams, 1978)

Burrow, John, *A History of Histories* (Allen Lane, 2007)

Chapman, Pat, *Curry Club Balti Curry Cookbook* (Piatkus Books, 1997)

David, Elizabeth, *English Bread and Yeast Cookery* (Viking, 1977)

—. *French Country Cooking* (John Lehmann, 1951)

—. *French Provincial Cooking* (Penguin Books, 1960)

—. *Mediterranean Food* (John Lehmann, 1950)

Davidson, Alan, *The Penguin Companion to Food* (Penguin Books, 2002)

Grigson, Jane, *English Food* (Macmillan, 1974)

—. *Fish Cookery* (David & Charles, 1973)

—. *Vegetable Book* (Michael Joseph, 1978)

Lee, Christopher, *This Sceptred Isle* (Penguin, 1998)

Montagné, Prosper, *Larousse Gastronomique: The World's Greatest Cookery Encyclopedia*, ed. Jennifer Harvey Lang, third English edition (Clarkson Potter, 2001)

Odya Krohn, Norman, *Menu Mystique: The Diner's Guide to Fine Food & Drink* (Jonathan David, 1983)

Saulnier, Louis, *Le Répertoire de la cuisine*, tr. E. Brunet, seventeenth edition (Leon Jaeggi & Sons, 1982)

Shaida, Margaret, *The Legendary Cuisine of Persia* (Interlink Books, 2002)

Smith, Drew, *Modern Cooking* (Sidgwick & Jackson, 1990)

Swinnerton, Jo, *The Cook's Companion* (Robson Books, 2004)

Tannahill, Reay, *Food in History* (Penguin Books, 1973)

Wilson, C. Anne, *Food and Drink in Britain* (Constable, 1974)

Index

*Please note that page numbers in **bold** refer to the main entry for a type of food.*